Hardin J Burlingame

Tricks In Magic

Hardin J Burlingame

Tricks In Magic

ISBN/EAN: 9783741152269

Manufactured in Europe, USA, Canada, Australia, Japa

Cover: Foto ©berggeist007 / pixelio.de

Manufactured and distributed by brebook publishing software
(www.brebook.com)

Hardin J Burlingame

Tricks In Magic

ricks ✳ ✳

in

✳ ✳ ✳Magic.

TRICKS IN MAGIC,

ILLUSIONS,

AND

Mental Phenomena.

CHICAGO:
THE CLYDE PUBLISHING CO.
1895.

o THE READER:

The effects in this pamphlet are selected from among
those secrets that have become common property in the
magical field, and are given just as sent out by the vendors,
except that the orthography has been corrected.

THE COMPILER.

TRICKS IN MAGIC.

1   Handkerchief Multiplication.

Get two silk handkerchiefs and put each in a small paper tube, and place each behind ear and keep in place with a small piece of wax. Show silk handkerchief and hand empty. Take handkerchief between hands by corners and lay over head. Take tubes from behind ear and produce in course of time.

2   Now You See it; Now You Don't; Handkerchief.

This trick although simple is one of the prettiest sleight of hand feats in existence. Use a fine small silk handkerchief, between the joint and thumb and forefinger of left hand conceal a small piece of the same silk rolled up in a ball. Roll up your sleeves, show hands empty, have handkerchief examined and taking it between the hand roll it up into a ball which you pretend to pass into left hand, but really palming it in right. Let silk at rear of thumb expand in left hand, letting audience see it, they are now sure that the handkerchief is really there; meanwhile you get rid of the handkerchief proper. In due time join hands roll up the bit of silk into a ball again and press it back in its former hiding place, then show handkerchief gone and hands empty. Cause handkerchief to reappear by

causing silk to expand and let it be seen, vanish‡
silk as described above.

---

3   **Soup Plate and Handkerchief.**

The handkerchief is rolled up very small and is hɛ
between the soup plate and hand, while the perform
is calling attention to the plate. When in the actɛ
laying the plate down, under cover of the plate drop ti
handkerchief. Vanish as follows: A small ball of aɪ
suitable material about an inch in diameter and withɪ
opening on one side of it about half an inch in diameɭ
is attached to a wire loop. This loop is slipped oᴡ
the thumb of the left hand. Performer takes a smɪ
silk handkerchief and works it into the hollow ball aɪ
under cover of the right hand slips the rubber ball oᴡ
the hand and allows it to hang down at the back of lɛ
hand. Palms of both hands can now be shown emp‡
performer picks up soup plate in his left hand and ɛ
hibits the duplicate handkerchief underneath and holɭ
soup plate in his left hand and under cover of the plɛ
drops the handkerchief and vanisher on servante aɪ
carelessly calls attention to the back of the hands. Tɦ
can be done very quickly.

---

4   **Mephisto's Glass Cylinders.**   ¦

Effect—Two glass cylinders are shown and thɛ
placed opposite to each other on the stage. Performɛ
borrows a dozen handkerchiefs and has them all tied tɕ

6

gether; he then places them in either cylinder, as selected by the audience. Performer now commands the
handkerchiefs to vanish, which they instantly do, and
appear in the other cylinder which was previously shown
empty. These cylinders can also be used for the vanishing and appearing of birds, rabbits, liquors, flowers,
etc., etc.

Secret—Have a cylinder of opaque glass about two
feet high; also two shells of same colored glass which fit
over the genuine cylinder that has bottom in it; also
have two pedestals (imitation of marble), which are hollow; these are placed over traps in stage at each side.
Assistant under stage has a long rod on one end of which
is a wooden disc; this disc is a little smaller than the
inside of glass shells. Performer shows shell and cylinder together, then places them on one of the pedestals;
assistant pushes up rod from below so that disc is flush
with top of pedestal. Performer now places the other
cylinder (shell), on the second pedestal. He now borrows some handkerchiefs and has them tied together,
these he places in first cylinder and, on command to
vanish, assistant quickly lowers rod and disc (cylinder
containing handkerchiefs is resting on disc), down, and
quickly shoves it up into the shell on second pedestal,
from which the performer produces the handkerchiefs.
Performer steadies outer shell, by placing his wand
across top of it and bearing downwards, meanwhile addressing the audience upon some point of interest, while
assistant pushes up inner cylinder. Of course you must
have audience imagine that both cylinders have bottoms
in them.

7

Effect—You hand to audience for examination, thr
silk handkerchiefs; one red, one white, and one blu
Next you show the two crystal cylinders, such as is us
on gas jets. Have someone in audience to tie the co
ners of blue and white handkerchiefs together and r
them into a ball, which you place in one of the cyli
ders, and give to someone to hold. You next take th
red handkerchief and place it in the other cylinder, an
hold one hand over each end of cylinder, and away fro
your body. You now command the red handkerchief t
vanish, and instantly the cylinder is seen empty; han
are still covering both ends. Person holding the oth
cylinder removes the two handkerchiefs and unrol
them, and to their astonishment they find the red han
kerchief which had disappeared from the other cylinde
between the blue and white handkerchiefs, all being ti
together. Very effective.

Secret—After person has tied blue and white han
kerchiefs together, you request him or her to roll han
kerchiefs into a ball, rolling the white one inside of th
blue one, and place ball on a plate which you hol
On returning to stage you palm duplicate ball fro
under your vest, and drop it on plate and pal
first ball which you place under your vest. The ba
now on the plate is composed of three handkerchiefs, t
blue one being on the outside of the ball. Now take on
of the cylinders from table and place on plate wit
ball; going to someone in audience, have them pla
ball in cylinder and hold the palms of their hands ov
each end of cylinder. Performer returns to the sta

nd picks up red handkerchief and slips it through loop of "pull," which until now has been over left thumb. Now you take up the cylinder and place handkerchief in it and, holding palms of hands over each end of cylinder, you command handkerchief to vanish, at the same time raise hand a little from end of cylinder on the side which pull is, in order to allow handkerchief to slip out easy, which is drawn up your sleeve by pull, as you extend your arms a little; place cylinder on table and walk to person holding the other cylinder and have them remove ball, which they unroll and find the three handkerchiefs all tied together; red, white and blue.

---

6   The Chameleon Handkerchiefs.

Three silk handkerchiefs perfectly white, are given for examination; also a small sheet of paper, all of which is found to be free from deception. The paper is then rolled up in the form of a tube, the three handkerchiefs pushed in one at a time, a few "passes" and the paper is unrolled, when the handkerchiefs will be found to have changed to red, yellow and blue.

Secret—For this trick you have a tin tube 3 inches long 1¼ inch in diameter; also a piece of white paper 8 inches square, and six handkerchiefs; three white, one red, one yellow and one blue. The three white handkerchiefs are laying on your table, also the paper for cone. Under paper have the tube prepared as follows: Cover the tin tube with one end of

the red·handkerchief, and sew it nicely, so that wi
you take the red handkerchief out of paper cone,
tube hangs behind the handkerchief. You tuck the
handkerchief into tube first, then the yellow o
then the blue one, and all is ready. To perform, st
the three white handkerchiefs one at a time, to pr
that they are unprepared; then lay them on your ta
and take up the paper. The three white handkerch
conceal the tube that was under paper. Show pa
and roll into a cylinder, then take up a white handl
chief at same time the tube containing the colo
handkerchiefs, which is not noticed by audience as i
concealed by white handkerchief. Get the tube i
the paper cylinder behind white handkerchief, in
act of pushing in the white handkerchief. As il
pushed in, out comes the blue handkerchief. N
push in second white handkerchief and out comes
yellow handkerchief, then push in the last white ha
kerchief and out comes the red handkerchief, allon
it to hang over the paper cylinder, then catch it r
top of cylinder and pull it out, tube and three w
handkerchiefs are drawn out as the tube is sewed to
handkerchief, lay it on table, no one suspecting the
handkerchief contains a tube and three white hand
chiefs, now open paper and show it is empty. Ano:
method of loading tube into cylinder is as follo
Have a fine wire loop attached to one end of tube,
concealing tube under vest at bosom, allowing loo
hang out. In the act of showing the paper (which
hold in both hands), catch thumb of left hand
loop, and as you start to convert paper into cylin

ecretly pull tube into same. And still another method
i to have the tube concealed on back of chair, and
hen you show white handkerchiefs throw them over
ack of chair, then show paper and make it into cylin-
er, taking up one of the white hankerchiefs you se-,
retly take tube with it and push into cylinder, etc.

New Postal Card Trick.

First take a postal card and prepare it with writing,
hen fold it twice, but before folding tear a square cor-
er off, place the folded card in one of your vest pock-
ts and the corner in the other. Now fold your card in
he middle lengthwise once, and then fold in the middle
rosswise once. When you wish to introduce the trick
how committee a clean card, while they are looking at
t palm your prepared card and corner, then take the
ard from the committee, hold it up so audience can see
t and tear off a corner as near the shape as you can to
repared one. Now ask one of the committee to fold
he card and while he is doing so give the prepared cor-
er to one of the committee and get away with the
lean corner, now take the folded card from person and
while showing it to audience exchange for the prepared
ard and place this in someone's hat with a lead pencil,
hen request spirits to write, after a few moment's request party to take the card and see if there is any writing on it. Let him read message and match corner to
he one other party holds and it will, of course, be found
to fit exactly.

8   **Cards Nailed Between Boards.**

Take 3 cards and blacken their backs. Now fo
small tack through each card, so that point is o
back. Lay them on table with backs up. Take tw
dinary boards; have them examined. Lay board
table, the bottom one over the cards. Get hammer
nails and give to someone. Pick up boards (cards
stick to them) and place them together, so that c
come between and have them nailed. Force 3 c
similar to those between boards and proceed with th

---

9   **Demon Cards.**

For this experiment you require two packs of pl
ing cards, one an ordinary pack and the other a
pared pack as follow: Take an ordinary pack and
a small piece off the end of each card. When all
cards are cut this way the pack will be a trifle sho
than an ordinary pack. Have this pack lying n
your table where it will not be noticed. Performer
attention to the ordinary pack and hands it to any
son and instructs him to go among the audience
have any amount of cards selected. Pack of cards
then returned to performer, who walks back to the t
for the purpose of getting a glass tumbler and he secr
exchanges the prepared pack for the ordinary p
these he places in the glass goblet and has any per
go through audience and collect all the cards which
drawn, and shuffles the pack. Cards are then pl

performer's pocket and he at once produces all the
rds drawn. All he has to do is to select the cards
at are a trifle longer than the balance of the pack.

Pipe Trick.

Take clay pipe, fill up with wadding (cotton wadding)
osely and keep in place at mouth of bowl by a wire
reen. Wet cotton with gasoline. Prepare soap water
d make soap bubbles with pipe. Let float in air and
ht bubbles with candle, they will explode with a big
me.

The Wa-Ha-Gi-Billiard Ball.

Over the billiard ball fits a half shell of glass, under
e cover of the handkerchief the solid ball is palmed
vay while the spectator holds the glass shell, which
ien dropped into the water turns over and remains in-
sible. The bottom of the glass is just large enough to
ceive the shell. To hide the edge of shell two stripes
e etched on the glass.

Magic Die, Flowers and Glass Box.

Have a three inch die and glass box made so you
n place the die inside the box. Also have a handker-

chief made by sewing two handkerchiefs together,
stitching between the handkerchiefs five pieces of s[
cardboard which are the same size as die.   The flo
are spring flowers same as used for paper cone,
are fastened on back of handkerchief with a th
Thus prepared place die in handkerchief and taking
of cardboard in handkerchief let die drop onto sen
and place handkerchief over box and make the m
as if trying to get the die in glass box, while doi
break the thread and the flowers will fill the box, ren
handkerchief quickly and the die has vanished,
audience see flowers.

13　　　　　**Ice Freezing Extraordinary.**

A square tin box is brought on the stage and pl
on a skeleton frame, shown empty and where it ren
during the entire experiment. It is then filled
water and covered with a thin cover.   A candle is
placed under tin box, about the centre and remains
a few moments, then cover is removed and a large
of ice, nearly filling the box, is taken from box.
ice may be either broken and previously borrowed
cles found imbedded in it, or ice for making lemo
(magically).

Explanation—Box is made on plan of Inexhau
box, i. e. bottom double and works on hinges, show f
and set box on it, the box containing cake of ice.
box towards audience and thus show empty, tip tov
shelf and show bottom solid, etc. Water runs dow

ice, through hollow legs, into bottom of frame. There
re two holes in the real bottom for the water to pass
rough, these being near corners, over front legs, and
re concealed by fingers when box is turned forward to
now empty. Use faked pail having false bottom near
p to show full of water. Ice cannot entirely fill box,
s tin could not be tipped forward. Size ascertained by
ial.

----

4 New Programme, Ring, and Envelopes Trick.

Effect—A ring is borrowed, also a programme, and
ie latter is torn in two. Volunteer is invited on the
latform. Half of the programme is spread over the
and and the ring placed on it. The performer then
queezes up the programme and ring, and commands
ie programme to change into a series of envelopes,
ith the ring in the centre one, and this is found to
ave been done. Volunteer has to open the four envel-
pes before he finds the ring. Performer now repeats
ie trick with the other half of the programme, and
gain the ring is found in the innermost envelope, and is
eturned by the volunteer to the owner. The broken
nvelopes are then taken in the hand, squeezed up, and
ransformed into programme again. "Very elaborate
ffect."

Secret—The ring is changed on wand (old dodge).
'he first series of envelopes is perfect (made out of
imilar programmes, of course) and carefully sealed up
'ith dummy ring inside, concealed (say) in right

15

pochette, and (when programme is handed) taken
tween root of thumb and finger—forefinger. The
gramme is laid on the hand, the substitute ring
placed thereon under the thumb, all squeezed up,
envelopes produced—the programme is slipped i
pocket while the audience are gazing at the opening
the envelope. Lay great stress on the fact of each
velope being securely fastened, and ask the volunte
he can take out the ring without breaking the seals,
etc. Meanwhile arrange for the repetition of the tr
The second series of envelopes is open at one end,
has a flat thin tube (a la shilling in ball of wool) d
into "not quite" the bottom of the smallest one
tube to fit loosely), and place each succeeding envel
wax side downwards. While the volunteer is wor
with the first set, drop the borrowed ring down the
into the innermost envelope (say in the right poche
shake the tube, withdraw it, then bend the ends of
envelopes over tightly, and proceed with the trick
the second half of the programme as before, asking
volunteer if he would like to do the trick.

A good finish is made by collecting all the en
opes, having a complete programme in the hand,
changing them for it. To do this simply squeeze up
bundle, bring the programme to the top, and han
over, immediately taking wand in hand.

---

15   Bertram's Programme and Coin Trick.

The program at the hall you are performing at sh
be (for convenience) printed on special paper. L

16

aper. Preparation for the trick: You must now get
ne of these programmes and cut it into four equal parts
nd make out of it 4 little envelopes so that they will go
ne into the other. Now borrow a marked quarter on a
mall plate and then get a gentleman on the stage to
old the plate and keep his eye on the quarter. Take
p the quarter in your finger and call attention to the
act that the coin is not for one moment removed from
heir sight, but left in full view on the plate. Just as
ou are about to put it on the plate, ring the change and
ave the substitute on plate and keep the marked one
almed. Now borrow a programme from any one and call
our assistant to bring you a stick of sealing wax, when
e comes on the stage and hands you the wax, you put
he marked quarter in his hand as you take the wax,
nd he at once goes off, places the coin in envelopes,
ne in the other, sealing them (sealing each one); per-
ormer now gives the programme to gentleman on stage
elling him to wrap quarter in it. While he is doing
his, the assistant places on table the envelopes and
hen walks off taking something with him. Performer
ow picks up wand from table and with the same hand
akes up the prepared packet and steps toward gentle-
aan saying: "That is not the way to wrap it; take it
ut again," and the performer then spreads out the pro-
ramme over his hand which contains the prepared
acket. Now let gentleman place quarter on programme
eneath thumb and crumple it up in hand at same time
alling attention to the fact that you double it up with
ne hand ONLY and as you do so gradually work the
arcel of packets up on to the top of programme that

you have just placed the coin in.   Quickly get it to
tips of fingers and let gentleman hold it in his h
You then take the sealing wax and strike the packet
times; then tell gentleman to unfold programme an
his surprise he finds an envelope sealed with wax,
he opens and finds another also sealed, then a third
a fourth, this fourth is given to the person of whom
borrowed the coin, and let him ascertain that it is
identical quarter he offered.   Now take the piece
programme in one hand while with the other you secr
palm a nicely folded programme then place the pi
on it quickly and squeeze them up into a ball in
hand.   Work the programme to the top, then to the
of fingers, and let gentleman unfold programme,
while he does so get rid of the pieces.   Show progran
is restored and hand it back to the person it was
rowed from, and end.

---

16   **New Chair Mystery.**

The performer is provided with a piece of black
thread made stronger by black wax.   One end is
tached inside the left leg of his trousers and the oth
attached inside his right leg of trousers.   The loop
made hangs down and touches the floor, but in a r
well lighted the fine thread cannot be noticed.   l
former takes the chair and after rubbing his hands
it, causes the leg to fall into the loop.   He then b
away gently and the chair follows him, while he
tends to be throwing whole chunks of magnetism in

This is entirely new, being the invention of a European medium. (?)

———

17 How to Tell Numbers of Borrowed Watches.

All that is necessary for the performance of this trick is the knowledge of the number of one watch, which is supplied by a confederate. The trick is now worked the same as in reading "envelopes." When the first watch is picked up he reads off the number of the inside of confederate's watch case. He now opens the watch case and reads off confederate's number and then notes the real number which he reads for the next watch. The audience are requested to note the numbers as read and when the watches are returned the owners state that the performer has been correct in his assertions.

———

18 Slade's Wonderful Spirit Knots.

With this trick Slade very successfully duped the celebrated German Scientist, Prof. Zollner.

Secret—Have two cords of the same length and same kind, into which have your "victim" make three knots. In your sleeve you also have two similar cords without knots. The four ends of the last two cords extend as far as the ring you wear on middle finger of right hand, they are just pulled through under this. Take the knotted cords and place the four ends together, at the

19

same time secretly pull out the four ends from un,
the ring and place them over the end of the first cc,
so that first ends are hidden by hand, while the spec-
tor believes the visible ends to be the ones belong
to the knotted cords. Have these visible ends seale:
the table top or to a card, using if possible a strang
seal, move hands towards the rear and downwards,:
the cords pull out of the sleeves. Take the knot
cords bunch them up and get rid of them, in due t:
spectator finds that the knots have disappeared fr
the cords. This experiment should be skillfully |
formed and proper mise-en-scene arranged for it, by
versing the process you can cause knots to appear
one or two cords that were apparently sealed to ta
minus knots. A table cloth pushed slightly towards
front of the table to make room for the sealing wor
more effectively hide the spiriting away of the first ce

---

19   **Dexters Sealed Cord Test.**

Have board three by five feet with two staples in
examined by audience or committee, board then pla
against wall, a box height of chair and placed THRE
INCHES FROM BOARD. The staples correspond
lady's neck, and about three inches above small
back. (?) Two gentlemen are chosen by audience,
tie lady, first gentleman ties string around lady's n
through staple, good knot solid and secure. N
gentleman ties string around lady's wrist (right w

and passes string through staple to other gentleman at the same time lady catches up a little slack of string and pushes her hand down behind her and below the staple, gentleman then pushes lady's left hand back and ties the other end of string around her wrist, all ready, gentlemen leave the stage. A plate is placed on lady's lap, glass of water placed on plate, curtain drawn in front of lady. Lady can reach and get glass and drink water, taps foot, curtain drawn back, audience see glass empty, (also hears glass placed back on plate) next handkerchief is tied around lady's neck, (lady used one hand and teeth to tie knot) other tests, etc., etc. Performer with a knife cuts string which is around lady's neck, lady bends forward and then cuts lower string close to hands and lets the piece of string drop behind the box. Lady steps forward and holds up hands to audience to examine knots, etc.

Whoever named the above, "Dexters Sealed Cord Test," knew nothing whatever of Dexter, because he never used any such kind of a tying feat.

_____

20   **Bellachini's Cabinet Mystery.**

Preparation—Make a large sack of dark flannel, 7 feet long by $2\frac{1}{2}$ feet wide. Cut two small holes two inches apart at back of sack, and as high as your wrists when standing in sack. Have four pieces of tape, two pieces one and a half feet long and two pieces one and a quarter feet long. Commence by asking two persons to

step upon the stage and allow them to examine the
have the two small pieces of tape in your pocket w
you can get at them quickly. Next show the 1
pieces of tape and request the persons to tie a 1
around each wrist and seal the knots, you now get
the sack and while getting in you must manage to
the tape out of your pocket and stick them through
holes in sack, and have them tied and sealed, it
now appear as if your hands were secured. Pieces
tape are tied, you now get in to cabinet and have
tain closed, and you can ring bells and blow horns, e
etc. Then curtain is opened and knots examined. 1
ask one of the committee to step in the cabinet, have
eyes blindfolded, curtain closed, then you turn his c
inside out, take off his collar, etc., and then get h
into position and have curtain opened; this make
laugh. When ready to finish your act have knots
amined, etc. After the person has untied the t
quickly pull them in and put them in your pocket i
pull out hands, showing wrists as tied at first.

Whoever named this act, knew nothing about Be
chini or his work. He never did anything in this li

---

21   The Three Knotted Charmed Handkerchiefs

Can be introduced into either light or dark sean
or where hands say are handcuffed behind back, or i
similar manifestation. First method: Is to bor
three handkerchiefs, have them tied up, or your assi

ant pulls the knots into the required slip knot, (the old knotted handkerchief "fake") and a simple pull with them of course separates them. He simply hangs them on top of screen or in front of you, or cabinet in which you are manifesting, or he can throw them over to you, in either case you pull them apart. Tie one around each arm at elbow and third around head, slip hands into bonds again as you call for cabinet to be opened. Second Method: Is to use your own handkerchiefs of which you have duplicates, the moment you receive the knotted ones which in this form may be knotted up in all sorts of form or ways by audience, or better still while assistant is making an observation. Before handkerchiefs are thrown into cabinet you free yourself and tie duplicates in the required position, and when you receive the knotted ones pop them into pocket, slip into bonds and have cabinet opened as you do so.

---

22 The Eglinton Rope Test.

An excellent rope tie, much used in England. Performer comes out with a piece of rope which he has some one tie around his wrist very tight, knots sealed, ends of rope tied to chair back and sealed. Use cabinet or canopy, doors closed and tests occur. Medium has a blade of knife sewed at back of trowsers and cuts the cord right through and produces from his pocket another rope similar to the first one, "faked" as follows: have a piece of rope same length as the one in hand when com-

ing before the audience, tie two single knots about [
or four inches apart which will be two inches from
centre, have these knots sealed with wax, now t[
double knot on rope, tying ends together and have[
knot about one inch or so on each side from the si[
knots, have sealing wax on this knot also. Perfor[
takes particular notice how the first rope on his w[
are sealed and so he seals the knots, while the lectu[
going on and can be done quickly. Medium then p[
ends through back of chair and fastens rope as the t[
one was fastened then sits down in chair, thrusts[
hands through the large loop gives his hand a tw[
around so that the two single knots meet between t[
two wrists and these two knots being sealed separate[
pear as one, when wrists are together, and the two kn[
appear as one good knot. Lights up, inspection follo[
and medium found securely tied. Conceal first rop[
gentleman from audience cuts the rope to show all th[
or release yourself and disappear through back of canop[

This is also mis-named, Eglinton, the medium, [
not use rope tying feats.

---

23   One of the Davenport Rope Ties.

Use a common wooden bottom chair with two hol[
at back of seat. Rope used is about two yards lon[
and tied around one wrist up as far as possible, bot[
hands then placed behind back and wrists tied togethe[
performer holding his arms as straight as possible, [

24

hat the rope is tied well up on wrists; then performer
teps into cabinet and ends of rope are pushed through
ioles in chair and secured, door closed and work com-
nences. The cord being well tied up the performer's
vrist, by slacking the hands he can easily squeeze out
if the knots. From position behind it is impossible to
ie hands so that one cannot be gotten out, one out he
iackens the other knot and hand slips out. When
nanifestations are through he appears with rope in his
iands and says he will be found tied up as the audi-
ince tied him in the space of one-half minute, while
ialking he folds rope up in hands and at the moment
loor is closed he changes it for another concealed rope
if same kind tied in a double bow knot, loops being in
ihe centre. By pulling ends, loops become smaller and
iighter on wrists; he ties ends under chair, slips hands
ihrough loops giving one a full turn around and holding
arms and hands as at first, he appears similarly bound.
Inspection follows.

---

24   **Braid and Tape Test.**

Take a piece of tape about two feet long in your
hand and call up two gentlemen out of audience to tie
you up; after they come up you go into cabinet and sit
down on the chair, which is a common spindle chair
with the spindles running up the back, so when you sit
down on chair give them the tape to tie around your
wrist, they will tie it the same as vanishing knots. After
they have tied one wrist you ask them what kind of a

knot is this, at the same time pulling on one end
tape thereby converting it into a slip knot. Nex
put your hands behind your back and at the same
run the other end through the back of chair, an
them tie it to the other wrist, expanding it as mu
possible, for it gives you more room to work the l
back. You should always have two or three piec
tape in your pocket tied with a slip knot, for if
should tie you too tight, you could break the tape
put it in your pocket and place one of the other t
on your hands. Then perform your tricks such as
bell, showing your hands through hole in cabinet,
etc.

---

25   The Medium's Tie, Similar to No. 23.

Use street car cord and allow knots to be pulled
tight, which cannot be enough to give pain. Have
left wrist tied tightly, knot sealed and hands placed
hind back and in placing the hands behind the l
finger reaches out on arm catching hold of rope
twisting it once. The right hand is then laid on lef
that back of right wrist rests on front of left arm, r
is then tied to right wrist, ends of cord are pas
through hole of chair and tied. As soon as cabine
closed performer gives his right hand a half turn wl
releases it, tests occur. Performer wets his hand r
his tongue, puts it back in rope, gives it the necess
twist and he is tied again as tight as before. Will
little practice it can be done very quickly.

A piece of two by four scantling is brought upon the stage and a hole bored through it by a member of the committee at a spot where the auger has been started by performer. The scantling which is about four feet high is then nailed to the floor. Performer sits with his back to the scantling and his hands behind him. Two ropes are handed to the committee and they are instructed to tie each rope around each wrist of the performer. All knots are sealed and strips of court plaster are pasted around the rope, and they are drawn through the hole in scantling and a big knot tied to them at the back. Strips of court plaster are pasted around the knot and joined to the wood so that it cannot be moved. A spike is then procured and driven into the scantling. Two guy ropes are then tied around the spike and these are used to brace the scantling and keep it firm. A sheet is placed over performer and hands appear through openings. They ring bells and write messages to people in the audience. The committee pull sheet away and performer is found to be bound as at first. The court plaster strips are still around the knot. A large (dry-goods) box is placed over him and he does a few more wonders, all of a sudden he rises and yells, "Take it off," "Take it off," and they remove the box and find him free. The rope has been cut from him although in his position it would be impossible for him to do it himself.

Explanation—The scantling has had a piece taken out of it near the top, into which the bit, or a blade of a carpenter's plane is inserted. The hole for the rope is

cut a fraction of an inch beneath the blade. The
which was taken out to make room for the plane
is fitted back on top. When the committee man
the heavy railroad spike into the scantling it force
plane blade down through the rope and the perfor
hands are free and all work takes place.

---

27   **New Spirit Hand.**

This is for a private sitting with one man in ca
or dark room. The victim and the medium sit opp
each other at a round table. The medium says, "P
your feet on my toes, sir, now you could feel my feel
should move?" The victim says: "He can;" but
cannot. The medium's foot is quietly slipped out
very neat imitation of the toe of a shoe made of
and is held down by the victim's foot. While
medium is asking a few questions, a rubber han
pulled from the trowser leg and adjusted by a fa
long piece of steel upon the right foot. The opera
requires but half a minute, and then the medium s
"Now sir, place your hands upon mine, if I was to m
you would know it?" Spirit hand now appears
disappears, it will tap a tambourine hanging o
victim's head and will slap him in the face, etc. Fin
the medium releases the victim's hands, rises and will
piece of rubber used for the purpose draws the h
back to his leg with a snap.

The seance is over and the man believes.

28

Effect—Performer comes forward and, picking up
two trestles which are now on the stage, he walks to
foot lights to show that the trestles are unprepared; he
places the trestles in center of stage about six feet apart.
Next he places a board on the trestles and introduces a
young lady, and after making some hypnotic passes
over her, picks her up and places her on the board on
trestles.   He now removes the two trestles from under
board and, to the astonishment of the audience, the
board with lady on it is seen floating in space.

Secret—There is a curtain hanging at back of stage, it
is of a striped pattern, lines running up and down (dark
lines on light back ground). The two trestles we will call
No. 1, and No. 2.   Pick up No. 2 first, swing it around,
then do the same with No. 1; then place them in center
of stage, (well back), just far enough apart to allow
board to rest on them.   No. 1 trestle is unprepared, but
No. 2 has a wire fastened to it. The end of wire is made
into a loop and this loop goes around two nails, one on
each end of trestle.   The wire does not show as the
back ground conceals it, as it is a striped pattern.   The
end of wire goes to top of stage.   Now show the board
(which is a foot and a half longer than the lady used in
the illusion), and lay it across the trestles, getting end in
loop of wire on trestle, take a long stick and wave it all
round, over and under board, but you must guard
against hitting wire on end of board.   Now introduce
the lady and, apparently hypnotize her, then pick her
up in your arms and lay her on the board, (feet towards
trestle No. 2).   Assistant now brings in a leather pillow

from side of stage to which is fastened second wire, ning to top of stage; the pillow is placed under the head, at the same time get wire under the board. remove trestle No. 1, then trestle No. 2, and lady floating in space on the board and front curta dropped.

An improvement can be made on the above by ing the board drop to the floor when you remove tles. In order to do this it is necessary for the la wear a sheet-iron band over her shoulders under d also a sheet-iron band around the calf of each leg, w stockings. These iron bands are to protect the from being cut by wires, as one in this method is pl around lady's shoulders, when placing pillow under head, and the other wire is placed under her legs placing her on the board. Lady must make herself stiff, so that when trestles and board are removed will lay straight in space.

---

29   **New Spirit Pictures.**

Effect—Medium shows a wooden frame, on whic a piece of cloth, both sides of which are shown and is placed on an easel. A lamp is then placed bet cloth thus rendering it transparent, and impossible anyone to touch cloth from behind without being Lights are then lowered a trifle, a little music, an spirit picture is slowly precipitated upon the clot colors, this being visible to every one present.

30

Secret—For this experiment procure the following ingredients from some druggist: "Sulphate of Iron," for blue; "Nitrate Bismuth," for yellow; Sulphate Copper," for brown; make solutions separately of each, by dissolving a small quantity of each ingredient in warm water. Now make a solution of "Prussiate of Potash," and put it in a bottle Atomizer. Now with a brush for each color, make a picture, landscape, portrait or anything you desire, on a screen of unbleached muslin, when dry these are invisible. Show the screen and set it on an easel in front of cabinet, now slightly dampen muslin and place a lamp back of it on a chair, lower lights a trifle; your assistant or medium in cabinet takes the atomizer, and from behind sprays all over the back of screen with the solution of prussiate potash, which slowly brings colors out. Effect is wierd, and, although, perhaps not artistic, it is a novelty and is apparently done by unseen agency. Light being placed at back of screen, audience can see that no one approaches screen. A little music covers sound of atomizer. Always see that the atomizer is screwed up air tight before using it.

---

10   **Shrine of Koomra Samt.**

Effect—A large cage containing a small one is seen on stage. A person is placed in small cage, when he instantly multiplies into three distinct beings, i. e., his double, his astral being and himself.

Secret—The large cage is six foot high and three

and one-half foot square, standing on four small
with castors. Small cage is in centre of large cage,
is twenty inches square and same height as large.
Both cages have bars on all sides running from bo
to top. The large cage has red curtains in front
on both sides, all work on spring rollers. The l
ground of stage is dark green, and the large cage l
curtain at back of same material; behind this cu
are concealed gentleman and lady. When perfo
places the man in small cage, he pulls down red
tains in front and sides of large cage, gentleman
lady now let green curtain at back fly up, move tw
three bars aside, and step into cage replacing l
(This must be done quickly). Performer quickly
red curtains fly up, opens door of cage, and out
the three persons. If you wish you can have g
curtain on back of cage painted with black stripe
represent the bars of cage, in this case you do a
with bars at back of large cage, but you cannot l
cage around after trick, as you can do by using bar

---

31   Mysterious Cabinet of the Mahatmas or
Wonder of Wonders.

On the stage is seen a small round cabinet res
on a high pedestal. Performer comes forward and
vites a committee from the audience to come up on
stage and examine the cabinet; when they have finis
the examination of the cabinet they take seats all aro

and the performer closes cabinet door and also takes
seat with the committee and commands the spirits to
'en the cabinet door; instantly it opens and manifesta-
'ns take place.   Then the performer asks the spirits to
rn the cabinet around so audience can see on all sides,
i well as committee; instantly cabinet revolves around
'thout any one going near it.   Musical instruments are
'aced in cabinet and are played; a glass of water
'aced in cabinet disappears; an empty basket placed
i cabinet is filled with natural flowers; faces, hands
id spirit forms are seen in cabinet, in fact there is no
id to the number of tests that can take place in this
'binet and without a person going near it.

i Secret—The cabinet part is what is commonly called
'ie cheese box, it is the same shape only larger.   Cabi-
'et is placed on a pedestal.   There are two mirrors oc-
'apying about a quarter of cabinet, these mirrors meet
t the center post, and sides of cabinet being reflected in
'iese mirrors, audience think they see all of cabinet.

' Person who produces manifestations is seated behind
'iese two mirrors.

52   Spirit Circle Under Test Conditions.

' On a board the size of a table eyelets are carefully
'rranged at measured distances apart and in such a
'nanner that there are two for each sitter whether lady
'r gentleman, one for the right hand and one for the
left.   Beginning at any point in the circle a piece of
'opper wire is passed around the arm of the first sitter

through the eyelet in the board, around the other
through the other eyelet and so on to the
sitter. In this manner the wire is threaded th
and through, fastening each person to the board,
the neighbor on either side, in fact to the entire
The company including the medium being interla:
ends of the wire are tied together, the joint cover
with paper, then with wax and are sewed and t
desired and any seal is set on. Now the lights t
tinguished and the usual manifestations take plac
cret: The medium has on false shirt sleeves so
has to do is to slip out his arms as soon as the ligt
extinguished, then go through the various man
tions replace his arms in the sleeves and call for
Now all can be examined and of course is found
Then have some one cut the wire.

---

33   **Great Mahatma Miracles.**

This is an ordinary cloth cabinet, but then
platform four feet square. Lady sits on chair
manifestations occur whilst her wrists are secured
ribbons, and audience see her hands extending fror
sides of cabinet. The front of cabinet is made w
piece of round or oval shaped gauze in centre, this
allow audience to see her all the time. Secret,
two front legs of cabinet are hollow. Performer
audience for bunch of keys, bells ring, and key
brought from front of house. They place news

34

nside, with scissors, and beautiful designs are cut out. There are a thousand tricks that can be done. Traps n hollow front legs are hidden by tape running along n floor of cabinet. At the bottom of trap there is a very strong rope, and when cabinet is examined assistant below holds rope very tight, so no one can open it. Of course all the "miracles" are worked from under the stage by assistant.

----

34   One Way of Producing Great Mahatma Miracles.

The medium has a boy with her about 7 years of age and quite small. He crouches under her skirts and comes on with her, and is not noticed. She enters the cabinet and passes her hands through openings in the sides of the cabinet and her hands are held by a committee and all the usual cabinet work goes on, the boy rings the bells, plays musical instruments, etc., etc. The cabinet is made of some black material and the transparent gauze is of some light color. The boy is dressed all in black, a la Black Art.

The originator of this wonderful (?) idea should receive a leather medal for his inventive genius ! ! !

----

35   One Method of Materialization and Dematerialization.

The test is done by using white silk used to sift gunpowder.

One yard of this silk can be carried in an ord
thimble, and five yards may be carried in a watch
A face made of rubber, painted with luminous |
It is blown up the same as a toy balloon but retaii
shape of a face. The whole affair is concealed
half inch gas pipe running into on the stage unde
flooring. Assistant works the bellows from behin
scenes. The spirit, (rubber face and silk sack)
forced up out of the gas pipe end by the air pu
into the silk sack.

---

36   Kellar's New Karmos.

Effect—On the stage is seen a platform with
feet. On this stands an ordinary looking chair.
lady sits down on the chair facing the audience, ar
securely blindfolded by the performer, who then m
some magnetic passes over her. He then passes ar
prepared pack of cards out for examination and
them shuffled. Going back to the stage, he stands;
hind a small table, and, holding the cards so that t
face is turned toward the audience, he draws off
card after the other and throws it on the table, the
naming each card as soon as it becomes visible. I
the next test he borrows a banknote and with it w
to a blackboard on the stage; the lady dictates to
the value and the number of the banknote, he wri
it down on the blackboard. He also borrows a ch
and the lady states at what bank it is payable,
made out the check, who is its owner, what the am

, etc. A spectator next chooses a word out of an un-
bridged dictionary and asks the lady what the word is
and she instantly tells him and describes the word. Another spectator writes a couple of numbers on the black-
board, brought down in the audience by the performer;
the lady instantly squares and even cubes the number.
For the final test some one writes four rows of figures
on the blackboard, each row containing four figures.
The lady audibly adds the numbers and dictates the result to the performer, who then carries the blackboard
away to the front of the stage and she now adds the
rows in any manner desired, that is, from right to left,
up and down, etc. She also mentions any number
struck out or touched by the performer.

The secret of this seemingly remarkable performance
is a very simple one. Everything that the performer
does is seen by an assistant behind the scenes, who
tells the lady what to say by means of an invisible
speaking tube, which consists of a rubber hose, passing
from behind the wings, underneath the floor up to the
platform, the rear leg of which is hollow. There is a
small opening here on which the rear leg of the chair,
which is also hollow, rests. The chair used is a cane
seat one, of the kind known as "Vienna Bent Wood"
Chairs. The rear leg of chair is hollow, also part of the
seat of chair, also spindle in back of chair where connection is made. The lady who enters from the rear
does not show the back of her dress, on which is fastened another tube, leading up to her ear and hidden by
her hair, which hangs down loosely. Under cover of

37

making passes over her the performer connects the|,
on her back with the crosspiece in back of chair, |
completing the connection. Anything spoken by|
assistant into his end of the tube, which has a mo;:
piece there, is heard distinctly by the lady. The r;
easy. The assistant sees the faces of the playing c;
and tells them to the lady who calls them off. The;
former holds the banknote in such a manner against|
blackboard, which is turned slightly sideways, that|
assistant can read its number and value by means|
spy glass, same with the check. In the dictionary|
the performer requests the gentleman to ask the|,
what the 10th word on the 35th page is. The assis|
who has a duplicate dictionary, hears this, looks|
word up and tells it to the lady. The squaring|
cubing of two figures is done by means of assistant;
ferring to a table of numbers, already squared and cu|
before the trick, the table including all numbers h|
1 to 100. The adding of four rows of figures w|
easily understood now. Meanwhile the assistant con|
the four rows and the performer now moves the bk|
board to the front of the stage, thus bringing it out of|
assistant's range of vision; but as the assistant|
copied the figures, he can tell the lady what the re|
of adding the first row comes to and any other ques|
pertaining to the figures. The trick of the lady tel|
any figure touched by the performer is one of prearra|
ment, the lady and performer having learnt by hear|
number of figures, which are touched and called of|
the lady in their regular order. The performer t|

38

akes some more passes over the lady, under cover of ꞁich he disconnects the speaking tube and then re- oves the blindfold from her eyes. She bows and aves the stage but does not show her back.

---

7   Silent Thought Transference.

A lady (or gentleman) while blindfolded tells the suit nd value of any number of selected cards, solves arith- ꞁetical problems, gives numbers of borrowed bank notes, ells time by any watch, describes borrowed coins, gives ꞁroper names as selected, and many other tests.   All his is done in absolute silence and while the lady is un- ꞁble to see, and can be entirely surrounded by any com- nittee.

In this feat of Silent Transmission of Thought, there ꞁs used what is known as a Silent Code.

The principles and details of this Code are easily ac- quired and are so fully described in the following that they may be readily understood.   There being no elab- orate code to learn it will be seen that this method does not require as much application and practice as sys- tems in which certain codes and signals have to be mem- orized.

By means of this code all the usual effects generally exhibited at Thought Reading Seances, can be repro- duced.   The medium is completely blindfolded and if

necessary can be surrounded by a committee from,
audience, to see that the medium is not connected:
the performer in any way and that he does not make
queries of the medium or signal to her.   Performer
not change his position at all. |

It consists in both medium and performer com
mentally and together. It is a known fact, that
beats for "common time" are always the same in m,
therefore with little practice it is easy for two per,
starting on a given signal to count at the same time
rate, and when another signal is given to stop, an
course they will both have arrived at the same num
This then is the actual method employed in this
and from it you will see that any number from 0 to 9,
be transmitted by the performer to the medium; w
of course is all that is required. It is best to exp
ment and find out what rate of counting best suits
two persons employing this code, but the following
gestions are offered: It may perhaps be best to c
mence counting at a slow rate; then gradually incre
until you find advisable to go no quicker, and then
here to one rate and always keep it.

Say you have in the room when first practicin
loud ticking clock, with a fairly slow beat, on the g
beat or signal you both start counting at the same
as the clock, of course the clock must be removed w
the rate has been well learned; or count at the ra
"common time," viz: 1 and 2 and 3 and 4 and so
or practice with a "Metronome," such as is used du
piano practice for the purpose of setting time and i
course. made adjustable. A very good rate to fi

40

ιdopt is about 70 to 75 per minute. Whatever rate is ound to suit best must be adhered to, you will find at ιhe rate mentioned any number up to 9 can be transmit-ιed with absolute certainty, after an hour or so of prac-ιice.

Now that the principle has been explained, the next items are the signals to be transmitted to give the medium the cue when to start, and when to stop, counting mentally.

Coin test—Say the performer has borrowed a coin the date of which is 1862, the first figure of the coin 1 and 8 are generally understood as most coins in use are 18 something or other, if of date 18 in the hundreds, then the performer must advise the medium of this by means of a wording of reply to the person who lent the coin, which can easily be arranged to suit one's fancy. The 6 and 2 have therefore to be transmitted. The performer stands away from medium or amongst audience. The medium being on the stage securely blindfolded, performer takes his position with chalk in hand in front of blackboard; holding coin in other hand. He does not speak a word but simply looks at coin, after a pause, the medium calls out: "The first figure I picture is a one," or words to that effect, now immediately the lady stops speaking they both commence to count mentally at the rate agreed upon by practice. In this case the number to be transmitted is 6; as the last word of sentence is spoken they commence mentally 1-2-3-4-5-6; during this short period the performer glances down at the coin as if to verify what the lady has called out, as soon as they reach the figure "6" the

41

signal "stop" has to be transmitted. This is do
the performer putting down on the blackboard sh
the figure called out by the lady, viz.: "One" (1)
will be seen by this method that the signal is quite
to transmit and it is perfectly natural to put dow
figure on the board quickly and sharply. The
figure of the coin is now known to the medium, the
figure "2" is transmitted in the same manner a
previous figure, the lady says the second figure I s
"8," as soon as she ceases speaking they commen
counting again 1-2, on the arrival at the figure "2'
performer puts down the "8," previously called
sharply on the board, which is the signal for "stop,
lady now knows the full date of the coin. The n
of the coin must be indicated to the medium previc
by the wording of the reply to the owner of the
after it has been handed to the performer, which
easily be arranged to fancy, the value of the coin c
equivalent number in the same way as the previous
ure and between the "6" and "2," that is, after the
has called out the "6" they commence to count foi
value, when an "0" occurs in the date, no pause is n
the performer putting down the figure on the boari
the "stop" signal immediately the lady stops spea
this if followed carefully will be found quite easy
natural in practice.

Any other system that one may adopt for givin;
starting and stopping signal can of course be ap|
but the method here proposed will be found to ai
the purpose, and cannot be detected.

The performer states to the audience that the

ill now tell the value and number of a borrowed banknote. He also states that the lady does not see the
numbers on the note in the right order and that he will
therefore make divisions on the black-board for these
numbers, supposing she sees a "3" first she would cry
out "I see a 3" and it belongs in the second place and
so on, till the full number has been called off.

Performer also states that she will first call off the
value of the note. Performer now borrows a banknote
remarking that he usually returns it. We will suppose
he is handed a $5 bill numbered 00481, he takes it
back to the stage and on the way there he looks at its
value, when the lady hears that he has returned she
raises her hand to her head as if in thought, at the
moment her hand starts to move, both count 1-2-5-10-
50-50-100 and so on, at the third beat, viz.: "5" performer gives a sigh, the lady then waits a moment and
says it is a $5 bill, while she did this performer has
looked at the third figure of the note, as it is understood
between them that she should first call out the third
figure of the note, which in our case is "4."

It should have been mentioned before that in the
banknote test the following order must be learned by
both performers previous to performance: 1-4-5-3-2 so
that now the lady has got to the $5 as mentioned above,
begin to count 1-4 in second time, on the second beat,
viz.: "4" performer will stop lady from counting any
further by slowly writing down $5 lady knows now that
the next number is "4" she however waits a moment
and then exclaims, "I see a 4 and it occupies the
third place," as soon as the word "place" is said both

again begin to count, now the figure in the first pla
to be called off next according to the pre-arranged o
this order is supposed to be 3d, 1st, 2d, 4th, 5th,
and so on, of course any other order will do as lo
both know it beforehand.   Now "0" is the same as
for the test, for when a number is not in the for
1-4-5-3-2 you must take the number to which wi
is added to it makes the number you desire, in
stance, for 7 take 2 plus 5 equal 7, for 6 take 1 pl
equal 6, 5 plus 5 equal 10.

So the third beat will be the one on which the
former will write down the "4" just called out. &
mediately the lady has said "place" both count :
and on the "5" the performer will write down r
quickly in the third place a "4" immediately the "
put down the lady knows that the next number acc
ing to the above arrangement which occupies the
place must be an "0," but she allows a second or
to elapse before calling it out, by this giving tim
look at note for next figure, by putting down a pre
number rapidly the lady knows that she has to a
to the number just communicated to her, which o
pies the second place, and so that he is ready to l
counting immediately she has finished her sente
then she calls out: "I see an '0' and it occupies
first place," immediately she says, "place" both c
for the "0" in second place, 1-4-5 on the 5 perfor
rather quickly writes down "0" in the first place, i
a moment or so the lady says, "I see another '0' an
occupies the second place," immediately on the '
"place" both count for the "8" 1-4-5-3, on the beat

44

3" the performer rather quickly, by this communicating to her that she has to add 5 to the transmitted number "3," writes down an "0" in the second place, then after a second or so the lady exclaims, "the next figure I see is an '8' and it occupies the fourth place, at the word "place" the performer deliberately writes down an "8" in the fourth place and the lady calls out, "I see a 1 and it occupies the fifth place," she could go on counting to herself as she would not know whether there were more figures or not, but the performer would next refer to the number being all right and she would know it was all over. $5.00 00481."

For black-board work: The performer asks any member of the audience to put down upon the board 4 or 5 rows of figures, usually composed of about 5 figures in each row, while this is being done, the performer informs the audience that he shall transmit the total of the columns of the figures now being put down to the medium. The sum having been put down on the board may something like this: 7234 the performer adds up first row quickly so as to 8679 arrive at first total of unit column, this, you 3201 will see amounts to 22 he has, however, only to 3795. transmit the 2 as amount to be carried is 6423 not necessary to be known to the medium, he therefore now takes the chalk in his hand and says audibly to the person who has put down the figures, "thank you," the lady who has been listening for the signal as soon as the performer ceases speaking they commence the mental counting to the transmission of the 2, viz., 1-2 immediately on the

repetition of the word "2" the performer draws a
line under the column of figures on the board, the
tap of the chalk on the board at the commence
the action of drawing the line, indicating to the
cease counting and call out the figure she had me
to herself when she heard the tap on the board,
she does, saying put down under the unit colu
7234 • figure "2," the performer glances
8679 column as if to verify what the lady ha
3201 out, but in reality to allow time to t
3795 the total of the second column, which
6423 added up during the time the lady was
——— ing, not forgetting to add on "2" carri
29,332 the first column, in this case it amount
the 3 has therefore to be transmitted, as soon
lady ceases speaking, viz., on the word two, as
they commence counting for the second column
case 3, they count 1-2-3, the performer then pu
sharply on the board "2" first called out by th
which is the cue to stop and then the lady know
the second figure is "3" and calls out according
proceed in this way until all the columns hav
added. This test is usually concluded by the pe
pointing in quick succession to any figure on the
which the lady calls out. This is simply an a
and is a pre-arranged order of certain numbers
the performer picks out as it were hap-haza
really in the order arranged beforehand. W
mean by pre-arranged order is to commit to me
set of figures; at the conclusion of the foregoing
performer points to 4 then 8 then 2 then to 1

46

)n, medium calling out figures as soon as performer :rosses it out with chalk.

Card Test—Have your cards memorized by their numbers: Ace 2-3-4-5-6-7-8-9-10, Jack 11, Queen 12, King 13, ask some one to select 7 or 8 cards. To illustrate the method, we will suppose he selects two of hearts, three of diamonds, five of hearts, seven of clubs, eight of spades, ten of hearts, ten of clubs, Queen of Diamonds, King of Diamonds, (nine cards in all), let him lay them in a row on edge of table (the edge furthest from you) while he does this take a look at them and notice which is the lowest card, convey the denomination (or value) of the card according to the following rule: Value is given by *laying down the card last named*. Count from the time last words leave lady's lips until the time the card is laid on the table, the number counted *to be added to the value of the card last named*, and if the sum is over 13 deduct 13 from it.

Suit is given by the manner of picking up the next card. Clubs, pick card up sharply and quickly giving it a kind of turn on table which will make an audible "scratch." Diamonds, draw the card slowly over the table towards yourself before picking it up. Hearts, make a thump when going to pick up the card. Spades, make the thump as if hearts but follow it by the scratch as in clubs. The value of the first card cannot of course be given by laying down the last card named, nor can we count from the time the last word leaves the lady's lips, as she has not yet said anything. You say "thanks" to the person who selects the cards and then

47

you both start counting; at the figure to be ind
make a "sigh," thus in our example above the
card is two of hearts, say "thanks" and count 1-2
heave a "sigh" or better still "breath hard," the
you indicated by picking up the card with a thump,
knows the first card, she names it and as soon
last word leaves her lips count again, now the ne
in value is 3 of diamonds, but we will skip this
to the 5 of hearts, you do not count 5 but only
last card named being 2 of hearts, 2 plus 3 =
heart is again indicated by a thump, skip the 7 of
and go to the 8 of spades, the lady says 5 of heart
you both count at 3 lay the card down with an a
rap lady adds 3 to 5 and knows the next card is a
the spade is given by the thump and scratch, the
can give the 10 of hearts by adding 2, then the Qu
Diamonds by adding 2, the King by adding 1. No
have skipped the 3 of diamonds, 7 of clubs and
clubs, this was done so that the audience may not
that the cards are given from low to high, you co
from the King (King is 13 plus 3 but according t
you deduct 13 leaving only the 3) for example if th
card had been a Jack and you wish to give a "2,
count 4 (Jack plus 4 = 15 minus 13 = 2, after givi
"2," you give the 7 of clubs by counting, of cour
ways indicating the suit by picking up the card; i
"thump," "scratches" and "draws" are really n
moves as motions should not be made un-natu
making them too pronounced, the practiced ea
easily tell them apart.

Chess Knights Tour. Patter—"We will now

luce what is known as the chess knights tour; for the benefit of those who are not chess players let me say that the knight is the little figure with the horse's head and it has the most peculiar moves of any figure used in any game of that class, it can go around the corner. The knight moves by starting from the field upon which he stands and going two fields or squares straight in any direction and then turning the corner and going one more field in some other direction. To illustrate (go to your black-board and point it out) if standing on say field 20 he could get to 35, (show it) to 37, (show it) to 30, to 14, to 5, to 3, to 10, or to 26, a choice of eight fields, providing he stood on a centre field. Now on account of this almost incalculable move it has puzzled mathematicians for nearly 2,000 years (chess is an old game) to know if that knight could be started here point to it) on field No. 1, and could be successfully led from field to field and yet never resting twice on the same field. After centuries of calculations this has been solved by a Frenchman and we will solve it again tonight for you, but we will make it just 64 times as difficult by not commencing on No. 1, as scientists always do, but on any field you may designate. Common sense will tell you that the knight's trip must differ in each and every case according to his starting point and we propose to make it a great deal more difficult by having the moves calculated out by our medium, who you are well aware is totally blind-folded." A number being called out by one of the audience you mark it out, the lady calls off the numbers and you connect the lines and mark out the field; at the conclusion your black-board will show lines running over it, stopping once on each square, but touching any square twice.

Explanation. The secret lies in this, that you m to your starting point, if you learn by heart the follou
(1)   18-33-50-60-54-64-47-32-15-5-20-3-9-26-41-5§
62-56-39-24-7-22-37-43-28-13-30-45-35-29-46-36-2§
44-27-42-57-51-61-55-40-23-8-14-4-10-25-19-34-49-
53-63-48-31-16-6-12-2-17-11-(1.)

You see it begins and ends with or at *One*, this r tion is all you need learn, suppose your audience ç 12 as a starting point, you say : 12-2-17-11-1-18-33-5 and so on finishing with 16-6.

---

38 New Silent Second Sight and Bank Note Te

The trick is performed as follows : The lady blindfolded and seated in a chair with her back to audience. She holds in her hand a slate or writes c blackboard, just as you please. You then in the mi of the audience say that you will convey to her date or number of words, etc., without sign or sig The lady is breathing gently and regularly, but so t you can see her and notice the heaving of her bu or shoulders. You then start her counting by drawi deeper breath than usual yourself. You watch breathing and she counts her breaths and so do and you stop her when she has breathed up to the n ber you want by again giving another deep breath. us suppose we want the number 74. You begin; lady is breathing regularly and you give a deep bre to start her so that as you ask for perfect silence can hear you, and as soon as she has heard your bre

50

she begins to count her own from the very next breath and when she has breathed up to the seventh breath you again give another deep breath, (just long enough for her to hear you) which tells her that the number is 7, and she goes on counting from that seventh breath and you again stop her on the fourth breath, when she at once writes down on the slate or blackboard "74." This is the principle on which the trick is worked. You will then understand that you can convey any figure, card or letter by the code. You do this in a drawing room or even in a hall if you can get your audience to be silent. But where she cannot hear you from any long distance, you have someone behind the screen or curtain to start her by making some little noise with the mouth, or anything else your fancy may suggest, but this person need not have the least idea of how the trick is done and any child would do for that. All the child has to do is to make a little hum or noise each time he or she sees the operator look at the article which he (performer) holds in his hand. This noise is to start and stop the lady when necessary and takes the place of the deep breath. The operator must remain perfectly still and not make any sign or sound but merely look at the article he holds in his hand each time he wants the little child to make the noise, as the child or whoever is behind looks through a small hole and can see the operator and is near the lady. Thus, say you want to convey the Queen of Hearts. You look at the card or paper on which the name is written and immediately the child sees you look, makes the noise agreed upon. You then count the breaths up to

twelve, when you look at the card again and imm
diately the child sees you look at it again, makes
sound. You then count the breaths up to three:
then look at the card once more, which stops the k
She then knows that the card is to be written d«
The Queen of Hearts is conveyed by fifteen brea
twelve for Queen and three for suit. Of course
see that you can convey anything if you only arrang
code with a number for each article. You must p
tice it when alone for a time with your subjea
assistant and you will soon learn it.

Dates of coins you only need convey as a rule
two last figures, as nearly all coins are of this cent
Numbers of bank notes, tickets or watches. Any c
from a pack, count the Ace as one and when you get
Jack count it as eleven, Queen twelve and King thirt
The suit will follow next by remembering that the (
is 1, Diamond 2, Heart 3 and Spade 4. Words by
following table:

1	2	3	4	5	6	7	8	
1—A	B	C	D	E	F	G	H	
2—J	K	L	M	N	O	P	Q	
3—S	T	U	V	W	X	Y	Z	

Thus the name "Blitz," is conveyed by:
Column   Letter.

1	2	Meaning first column and second
2	3	ter, second column and third let
1	9	first column and ninth letter,
3	2	so on.
3	8	This is learned without difficult;

a few minutes.

This is usually used for a hotel or press seance, i. e., for advertising purposes, and is claimed to be very striking.

The performer enters into conversation with some people in the hotel or office, wherever he happens to be, and makes the suggestion that his assistant's powers can be tested at a distance. One or more cards are generally selected, some initials may be chosen, a number in dice is thrown and a series of figures may be written down, dates selected and time of day noted. One or two gentlemen are chosen as messengers. They take any sheet of paper and envelope, with pen and ink and proceed to the assistant's room, wherever that may be, and hand her (it is generally a lady) the paper and pen, without saying a word, and in a few minutes she hands them a correct written answer to all their questions with necessary proper descriptions.

The manner of working this is as follows:

Of course you arrange with your lady beforehand just what you are going to do. In this case let us suppose one card is drawn, one dice is thrown, one number is thought of, one set of initials is written down, and the time of a watch or clock noted. Now to the lining of the side of your coat pocket nearest the hand with which you write sew two short pieces of elastic cord in such a manner that they will grip neatly a book of cigarette paper, such as you can buy in any cigar store, (see figure 1.) The book cover is doubled back so as to leave one of the sheets of paper on top of it. In the same pocket have a very short pencil not too sharply pointed so as

not to tear the tissue paper while writing on it.
your vest pocket have a common fountain pen. T
prepared you are ready to perform the experime
Under pretense that you are not going to handle
articles you keep your hand in your pocket most of
time, and this gives you a chance to jot down the
rious abbreviations for the answer. Of course what th
abbreviations mean yourself and lady must know.
this case the following are selected: card selected, K
of Hearts. Dice, a six spot. Number thought of, 4
Initials thought of, E. H. Time of watch, 9:31.

You jot these down as soon as selected and
course the difficulty of writing this way will not m
the bit of paper (figure 2) a good specimen of ca
raphy, but still it will be legible enough for y
assistant to know what each abreviation means.
knows that the first is a card, the second a dice, and
on. While the messengers are being selected, tear t
sheet off quietly and gently in your pocket and mak
little ball of it, palm it near the tips of the middle
index fingers, which is very easy to do. Take out y
fountain pen, and as you take off the cover part of
case which protects the pen and which is always put
the other end of the holder while writing, you slip i
it the little ball. This can be done very easily a
very little practice. Do this while the attention of
spectators is taken up with the messengers, (select
them). The trick now needs no further explanati
When the gentlemen knock at the lady's door, she i
course, prepared to receive them. She takes the pa
and asks them to kindly wait outside as the presence

strangers is irritating to her. She takes the ball from its resting place with a hair pin, smooths it out and translates the abreviations into plain English and then writes the answer on the letter head which the committee has given her. When this is done she opens the door and the gentlemen take back the answer, totally unconscious that they themselves carried the information as to what the answer should be. Dates on coins, birthdays, etc., may also be used. If you are a second sight artist you may use your numbers to indicate chosen articles.

Fig. 1.

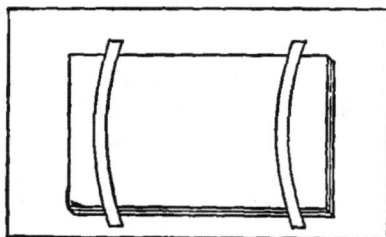

Fig. 2.

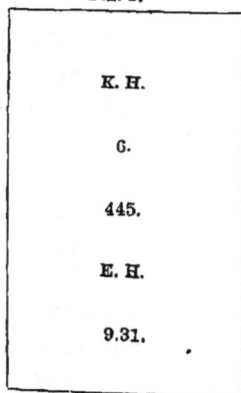

K. H.

6.

445.

E. H.

9.31.

Fig. 3.

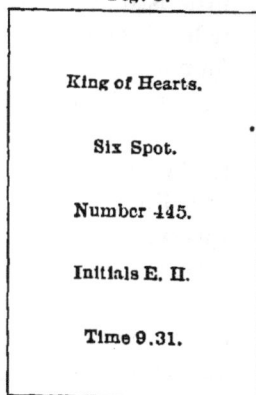

King of Hearts.

Six Spot.

Number 445.

Initials E. H.

Time 9.31.

As introduced by Prof. Verbeck and Mdlle. Math
in Paris and London and Guibal and Marie Greville
England and America.

Effect—The performer, or better say, the profess
as there are two performers actually, advances, and w
the seriousness of a hypnotist, announces the marvel
intuitive powers of his subject, Miss Venus. (?) "
shall be hypnotized by me, and when launched into
hypnotic sleep, can and will perform any rational
that the spectators desire, despite the fact that I (
professor) will not speak one word during the perfor
ance. She will while in this trance walk among
and comply with your requests. This the trance-it
Venus is, when I have her under control and in the h
notic trance, I will move about among you, and
can convey to me by whisper what you would wish
medium to do, and you will find she will not fail
aught of your desires." Miss Venus is now introduc
by the Professor, she is pale and has two lovely bla
eyes. (?) Her hair for effect is loose on her shoulder
she is robed in white, a Galatean costume. She bo
and smiles consumptively, and seats herself on cha
facing spectators. The professor now by means of ar
of the pantomimic gestures, pretends to hypnotize he
and she is or becomes hypnotized. (?)

Now performer goes among the audience, askin
here and there what the spectators would wish the lad
marvel to do, and having gone through say 12 to 20,
solemnly demands the strictest silence, and with seriou
mien advances toward medium without going on stag

and motions or waves his right hand in a downward movement in front of her. She slowly rises and goes through each performance desired, goes back to chair, slowly seats herself, and suffers (?) herself to be de-hypnotized, then the performer recapitulates for the benefit of all what each spectator desired and how Miss Venus was successful in each and every crucial test.

Explanation: In performing this seance the performer must learn a code of signs and things, these things the professor forces into the minds of the people.

Code to be learned for forcing:

1. Pull a gentleman's hair.

2. Turn up his trousers.

3. Tie a number of knots in his handkerchief.

4. Take watch out of gentleman's pocket and place it in another.

5. Open a lady's bag, take out her purse or anything she may desire.

6. From out of a number of coins placed in a hat, .pick out the special one which has been selected.

7. Write any number selected on a card.

8. Take a gentleman's cane or umbrella and put it in the hands of another gentleman.

9. Take glasses off a person and place on own nose.

10. Take off lady's (?) or gentleman's gloves.

11. Write down time by gentleman's watch.

12. Write autograph on programme gentleman holds.

13. Takes handkerchief out of person's pocket and ties it on neck or arm.

14. Ties a knot in watch chain, and so on.

This can be varied indefinitely as the reader ᵢ have already observed.

How to force these requests. The professor tends to hypnotize the subject, this as was said, sham, then going among the audience, he goes to ᵣ ber one, or first person, and asks this one wha would like her to do, he says, for instance: "Oh her tell me what I have in my pocket," or he would gest some similar test. Oh, says the professor, you get that she is hypnotized and we cannot have speak, get her to do so and so, or this, or that, or so so—and so the professor shoots out a volley of ᵢ gestions from his learned code rapidly, and ᵢ natural result, the person selects one of these suggest

Going to the next he forces differently, and ᵣ what shall she do for you? Turn up your trous. Pull your hair? Tie a knot in your handkerchief? ᵢ so on. The professor here springs a volley of quest before gentleman has time to make any suggestions mentioned by the professor, then seeing a lady sit near with a bag, he says: Madam, have you a pᵣ in it? Yes. Shall the lady remove it or anything from it? and so on. Again you see a gentleman ᵣ glasses on, and suggest that the medium move the sp tacles, etc. If, however, gentleman does not wish done, professor suggests some of the other tests, ᵢ etc. Remember medium's eyes are closed all the ti and in going through audience professor asks each i vidual his or her request in whispers only, and generally has each person whom he asks a coupl yards apart.

58

Again it is better when forcing questions to force only three at a time, and force them in rotation. To do this we should say he suggests three questions, but emphasizes or forces one of the three. Now, the professor has to keep his wits about him, for having gone to a sufficient number of audience, he must keep mental track of the gentleman who selected No. 1 of code, he who selected No. 2 and so on. When he goes to stage to wave down Miss Venus, all she has to do is to follow the professor in front or at side, and the first he stops at (by signal) she merely does first on code, the second he stops at, she does second on code and so on right through. The professor must remember where each chooser is seated, for example, suppose these lines are rows of people, and each word is numbered and represents those whom the medium has to go to.

The professor directs his medium to the person by the movements of his hands, he first shows her the rows in which the persons are seated, all the time waving his hands as if making mesmeric passes, and as medium is walking along the people very slowly, as soon as she reaches No. 1 performer drops left hand at his side, and the medium stops and pulls gentleman's hair.

Professor then directs her to No. 2 and she is then stopped again, and she turns up gentleman's trousers, and when she gets to No. 3 performer tells her how many knots to tie on handkerchief, by the number of downward waves of left hand, at the same time making passes with the right. To select any special coin

out of a hat or other receptacle, Miss Venus takes
in the hat in her hand, the right, and lets them drop
by one into the left hand, when she reaches the prop
article, performer turns to audience, as if silencing the
and says "hist."

Venus however continues pouring them into left han
and when all are in, she picks out the one she know
correct.

These methods may be readily varied to suit t
performer, who with a little skill and thought can wo
it up to most any extent.

Suppose something special and not in code is me
tioned to be done, you have to whisper it to medin
and to effect this whisper, when in the middle of t
test, you look around the audience, turning your ba
to medium, and you look as if you were looking t
some person who selected something, and medium wa
back to stage, you turn around, surprised to see t
medium away from you, and follow her up, wavi
arms and hands energetically, and walk slowly arou
her, this near the stage, and rapidly whisper what y
want to, at same time waving her back to audience, a
it were, i. e. you leading her, you have to walk dov
aisle backwards and face to medium. This of cour
can all be done while you remain on the stage with t
medium, together with a committee seated about t
stage, scattering your work among them, so as to avo
crowding about narrow aisles.

The medium's eyes appear to be closed all the tim
but in fact are open sufficiently for her to see all mov
ments of the professor. After becoming expert it w

not be necessary to use the forcing code often, because all requests can be whispered to medium by professor without the audience becoming aware of it. He can do this when he escorts her from the stage to the audience, or as he occasionally passes her in the aisles, and the waving of his hands and arms in his different "passes" will partly tell her what she is expected to do.

This so-called Hypnotic demonstration has proven to be one of the most puzzling effects that have been introduced for many years.

---

41 The Spirit Thinkephone, or Marvelous Vision.

In effect as follows: Performer walks into a newspaper office and asks someone to think of a card in an imaginary pack of cards, after he has done so to write the name of the card in his note book or on a slip of paper, and keep same in his pocket, then party writes a note asking name of card, and encloses note in an envelope which he seals and addresses to the performer's assistant. He then calls a messenger to deliver the note to the assistant at the hotel and return with answer; he does so and the answer is found to be correct. The explanation is as follows:—

There are four suits in a deck of cards, viz. Hearts, Clubs, Spades and Diamonds. Each of these commences with a different letter. Performer watches party as he starts to write name of card. Suppose for instance it is the five of spades. As soon as he sees the number 5 written down he watches to see what suit it will be. This he knows as soon as he sees the first letter put down,

which in this case is "S." He then turns his back
order to avoid watching the person finish writing t
name. The information as to what the card is, is co
veyed to the assistant by two finger-nail marks on t
envelope, one on the back and one on the front. T
front of the envelope is divided into 12 imaginary spac
(see figure 1). At one end of the back are the places
the marks to represent the suit, hearts, diamonds, a
spades (figure 2). If the back has no mark it is a cl
The front of the envelope represents the number of sp
on the card. One for ace, etc., eleven indicates t
Queen, twelve the King. If the card is a Jack th
will be no mark on the front. In this case the card
the five of spades. In picking up the envelope the p
former markes it front and back as shown in figur
and 4. Or the envelope may be marked after the m
is enclosed in it. This may be done under preten
examining it to see if the address is correct.

If required to repeat the test the performer may v
the modus operandi by addressing the envelope hims
and doing away with the fingernail marks. This is do
as follows: Take the first 13 letters of the alphabet
the initials of the person addressed and also let th
represent the 13 cards in suit.

A   B   C   D   E   F   G   H   I   J   K   L
1   2   3   4   5   6   7   8, 9   10 11 12

Now if you wish to communicate the card "10
hearts," the address on the envelope would be as f
lows:

Mr. John Smith,

Auditorium Hotel.

The initial "J" indicates 10 and the first letter of the place (Auditorium Hotel) coming under the first capital letter of the name indicates "hearts."

The suits of the cards are indicated by the capital letters in the name. The first capital letter means hearts, the second one spades, and the third one means diamonds. If no capital letter is indicated the card is a club. The particular capital letter you wish indicated ·has the first letter of the place addressed placed immediately under it.

Fig. 1.

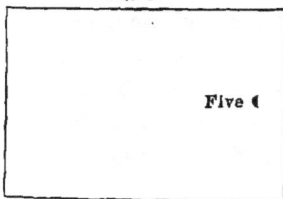

Fig. 2.

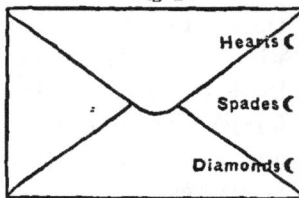

Fig. 3.

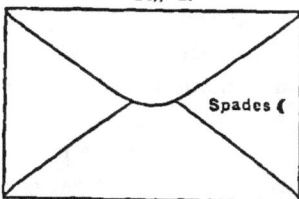

Fig. 4.

42 Tachypsychography, or Long Distance Second Sight.

A plain, ordinary kitchen table is brought upon the stage, and a committee of ten is called for from among the audience. The manager then says to the committee:

"Gentlemen, five of you please take the mind rea
outside of the hall and keep him in charge for half
hour." Five of the committee take the mind rea
outside while the other five watch the man on the sta
A watch is borrowed from the man in the audience. T
manager then asks one of the committee at what ti
he should stop it. The watch is stopped at 3 minu
past 12. The manager sees this and places it careless
on the table. A cigar case is borrowed and the man
ger asks for a number of cigars. The case is filled
partly filled with say 6 cigars or as many as the co
mittee decides on. The manager then carelessly h
it upon the table. He then asks one of the commit
to write the name of some friend, the first name on
upon a double slate, which is then handed to someo
in the audience. The pencil is then laid on t
table. He now requests the committee of five to ta
him outside and to keep him until after the mind rea
has finished. The committee does so and the mi
reader returns. He at once sees the watch and t
committee asks him what time it is by the watch. T
answer is 12.03, the watch is opened and the answer
found to be correct. He then tells that the number
cigars is six in the case and that the name on the sla
is Harry and the number in the sealed envelope is t
All prove correct.

Explanation—The table which must be a round o
is divided mentally into 24 parts, 6 in a row and 4 de
There are no lines upon it, but the mind reader a
manager have made a mental division of it with a p
in the centre to guide them, if they are a little clum

64

they can readily see any of the 24 divisions mentally, each square represents a name, 24 common first names. There is also an imaginary face of a watch upon the table, the XII being towards the audience and the VI being opposite. The watch is laid with the ring toward the audience which means 12 o'clock, it is laid in the third space marked off mentally, which means 3 minutes after 12, if it had been stopped at 12 minutes after 3 it would be laid on the right hand of the table. The ring would be pointed to the right, which would mean that the hour hand was set at 3, the 12th space indicates the minute hand. In case the watch was stopped 52 minutes after 12, it would be laid face downward, which indicates that the time is a half hour past the hour at which it is (laid) stopped, plus the spaces in which it is laid. The slate pencil is laid in the space marked "Harry," and the mind reader knows that Harry was the name written on the slate. The cigar case is lying in the 6th space and means that there are 6 cigars in it. The lead pencil is laid in the 9th space pointing toward the 4th place and indicates that the number is 94. If it was 944 an envelope thrown carelessly on the table would mean a repeater for the last number. Any number of tests may be introduced on the above plan. The committee are satisfied that there has been no collusion and their report is to that effect.

---

43   **Hypnognotism.**

The feat called Hypnognotism is in effect as follows: Performer introduces lady and after hypnotizing her,

blindfolds her, by placing a hood or bag of impenetr
material over her head, which fastens by tightenin
cord under her chin or around her neck. This ba
hood is examined beforehand, placed over flame of c
dle, to prove that it will not even show light throug
and is placed over spectator's head, who will vouch
it being impenetrable.

On the stage is a large easel, with large sheet
glass in an upright position. The glass is remov
and can be replaced by another sheet when necess
on a small table are crayons of various colors, ph
so the performer knows the place of each color, a
stick of soap with which to draw on the glass.

Performer announces that for the first test, he sh
like to have some spectator whisper in his ear the n
of any object, or design which he desires drawn by
dium, say an animal, flower, cross, anchor, face,
When request is whispered into performer's ear, for
ample; "draw an elephant," the performer faces
medium who rises from chair, takes up crayon and dr
the elephant. Performer does not speak one word
make any gestures, or even walk.

For second test performer says: "we will now d
in the same manner, a composite, or combination
ture, either a landscape, marine view, fruit pictur
anything else. Various spectators will please sug
the composite part of the picture."

He steps up to someone and asks: "shall it be a la
scape, marine or fruit?" Say a landscape is cho
He then asks another spectator: "shall we have a c
or clouded sky or a sunset?" Next he asks: "shall

have a mountain in the background," etc., until he has collected ten or twelve requests for the composite picture, like this for instance: landscape with lake, waterfall in background, 2 large trees in front, shrubbery, a road-way, fence, 3 ships on lake, birds in air, sunset, sky, etc., of course performer must take care that no one suggests ships when there is no water, or lighthouse in a country landscape.

The next test is a coin test.

Performer asks for a coin of any value and says the medium will draw it in yellow if gold, in white if silver, blue if nickle, red if copper, so as to show its value and date, then medium draws picture. It appears reversed on the glass.

The next test: A visiting card is asked for and medium steps over to glass, and standing behind it writes the name backwards, thus: htimS .N. J. It will read from front side of glass: J. N. Smith. The reason for doing this will be seen later on, but audience are told that picture or object seems to be reflected upon medium's mind as a picture in a mirror, and while that makes no difference in drawing flowers, since they appear the same, but it does make a difference in names and figures, that is why glass is used instead of paper in all tests where letters or figures are transmitted.

A watch is asked for and owner sets it at any arbitrary time. Medium draws it as if it were figures, that is, as it would appear in a mirror.

Number, series, and value of bank note is transmitted next.

If it happens to be anything but a U. S. Treasury

note, the name of the national bank is also included
number or figure is whispered in performer's ear,
lastly a word or name of a city or of an eminent ma
whispered to him and they are reproduced by medi
Other tests may be introduced ad libitum, such a
domino being selected and drawn, a word from a b
etc., etc.

Explanation—First to be explained is the bag or he
or blindfold. Get some black or very dark flannel a
crape such as used for widows' veils. First make a l
of flannel to fit over the head, neither too loose nor
tight. Now cut your crape in same shape, but abou
quarter of an inch wider and one or two inches lon
so as to fit over the flannel bag, making a hem fr
three quarters to an inch wide; through it run a rib
or string with which to tighten bag around neck, a
sew the hem to the flannel, but only half way arou
this will admit of putting head between crape and flan
as the crape is transparent, medium can see every mo
or motion of performer; when you are ready to use ho
prepare it by taking black thread, place into a nee
and at the end of the thread, before knotting, place
small black bead, then sew up the open side with lo
stitches and leave the bead on the inside; draw up u
bead is close to cloth, and cut off the thread on the oth
end nearest needle.

The hood will stand temporary examination, wh
performer turns with it to stage, he simply takes hold
the bead and can withdraw the entire thread with a
pull. The head of the medium is placed so he or s
can see through the crape and the string is drawn arou

the neck, this is the reason that the hem is only in the crape and not in flannel also.

While the medium can see everything, her face cannot be seen, when the proper kind of crape is used, neither too thick nor too thin; there must be no light directly behind the medium.

If one thickness of crape is too flimsy, use two.

The transmission of the requests of audience depends upon a kind of finger alphabet, or deaf and dumb language, there being several kinds, but the following method is most serviceable and if the performer uses judgment, no one will attach the least importance to it, and yet he will be able to transmit almost any desired word in five seconds.

The letters of the alphabet as well as the figures are given by playing with the watch chain, and the right hand alone gives them. Therefore, first let us say, that performer making his introductory speech or lecture, already should play with his chain, twist it around his finger, etc. The left hand has nothing to do with these signs, it is used to transmit other information.

Here are signs for the left hand first.

Code "A"—Left hand and arm hanging down by side: I am giving numbers. Left hand akimbo at hip: I am spelling something. Left hand at lapel of coat, near top button: I am giving abbreviations. If left hand moves slightly, say three inches or so, while in any of these positions: I am giving a color by its number. Shifting your weight from one foot to the other, means; I am starting or I am through.

This last sign is used in the following way: If per-

former .only kept his right hand at the chain when
essary it might arouse suspicion, therefore the med
must receive some signal when the performer c
mences signaling. That is done by standing with
legs a few inches apart, and shifting the weight of
body from one leg to the other, which gives a kin
swaying motion to the body scarcely noticeable to
uninitiated, but enough for the medium. When thro
giving signs, instead of always moving hand from
chain suddenly, which would also be suspicious, k
your hand there but shift your weight back to the o
foot, meaning, "all through," then even if you keep
the playing with the chain, medium knows that then
no further meaning to it.

Code "B"—Next we come to the signs of the r
hand. We will first explain the 10 figures: It is to
presumed that the performer wears a dress coat, v
a low cut vest and carries his watch in his lower
hand vest pocket, with the staple in second or mid
button-hole. It is advisable to have the chain sev
inches longer than usual length. The chain itself
nothing to do with the signaling, it is the right h
alone that must be watched by medium and on wh
ever portion of the vest the finger-tips rest, indica
what number is meant.

For figure 1, pick up chain at "X", its middle,
place fingertips against bottom of vest, directly in
perpendicular line from the watch pocket.

No. 2 Fingertips at watch pocket.

No. 3 Above watch pocket, near upper pocket. O
Two and Three are on the left side of the vest.

No. 4 At bottom of vest where the two parts of vest meet.

No. 5 At or near the staple.

Four, Five and Six are in the centre of vest, for cipher the sign is made by twisting the chain around right thumb, without the help of the fingers. The chain should generally be held by its centre when it will be easy to reach the various portions of the vest. For One, Four and Seven, go as low down as the chain will permit, for Three Six and Nine as high as you can.

Suppose you had to transmit 1892, which is whispered into your ear while still bending down to the person who whispered to you, you take hold of chain at "X" in an aimless way, and straightening up face the medium, let your left arm hang, which means, I am giving numbers, and when you see that medium is ready for you, shift your weight, which means, "begin"; at the same time place the right hand at One, that is, let the fingertips touch the bottom of the vest below the watch pocket, the hand must not be stiff. It can play with the chain, twirling it slightly, but it must be at One, leave it there a second or two and then slowly take it to Eight, do not make the movements jerky, but deliberately and aimlessly, and remember that no matter if the hand is held from above or from the side, the tips of the fingers must be at the figure, then follows Nine, that is, you simply bring your hand about two or three inches higher up, still playing, and then finally take it slowly and carelessly to the watch pocket, which is Two, never drop your chain suddenly, but shift your weight, which means all through.

The entire signaling should not occupy more t
from 5 to 8 seconds; with practice, 30 to 50 letters
minute which is about one word in 10 seconds can
communicated, long words may be abbreviated.

We now come to a description of the alphabet. 1
omit K and Q at first. A is made just as figure one,
as two, C as three, D as four, E as five, F as six, G
seven, H as eight and I as nine. Then we begin o
again: J is one, L is two, M is three, N is four, 0
five, P is six, R is seven, S is eight, T is nine, but l
these letters J to T shake the chain a little, while
former case, A to I, hand is held almost quiet, twirl
the chain slightly will not give a decided motive, shak
the chain gives a decided up and down motion to t
hand and is distinctly visible even at 50 or 60 feet d
tance. Care must be taken that the finger tips rema
near the places one, two, etc., and not midway betwe
any two numbers. Practice before a mirror, so as n
to get the habit of looking at the hand, and see that t
movements look careless and not stiff, jerky or violen

The letters U and W are given same as cipher, b
twisting chain around thumb, describing a circle wit
hand, but in U, circle is made at 4, 1, 2 and 5 that i
on the lower left side of vest, in W it is made at 5, 2,
or upper left of vest. The remaining letters K and (
are given by twisting chain around first or index finge
this will make the circles go in the opposite direction.

The remaining letters are given by a kind of whip
movement.

Grip the chain tightly between first and second finger
and thumb, and make a stroke up and down, as if th

72

chain were a whip. This will give to the hand a kind of violent up and down movement. If made in centre of vest and only once it is a Y, if near numbers 4, 5, 4, if twice in quick succession it means Z. If at watch pocket twice, 1-2, 1-2, it means X.

This alphabet should be thoroughly learned and diligently practiced, using small words to start. To show where one word ends and the next one begins, drop chain from right hand, remove hand three or four inches and then pick it up again at X for next word. Don't forget to shift your weight at beginning and end of sentence. If figures are mixed in with words, for example, house with three windows, drop your left hand at end of "house with," to side, and make the three, then raise it again to hip and spell the next word.

Code "D" Colors—No. 1 red, No. 2 white, No. 3 blue, No. 4 black, No. 5 brown, No. 6 yellow, No. 7 gray, No. 8 green, No. 9 silver, No. 0 gold. See code for color signs of left hand. Take a complicated example, white house with red doors, and three yellow windows. Play with chain until ready, left hand at hip, "spelling," shift weight, "ready," bend elbow back, "giving figure 2," which means color 2 or white, elbow forward and drop chain, "end of word," pick up chain and spell "house," drop chain, "end of word," bend elbow back, "color," pick up chain and give No. 1 meaning color 1 or red, elbow forward again, drop chain, pick up again and spell door, drop chain, end of word. Drop left hand to side, giving figures and make 3, raise left hand an inch or two, which means color in that position, (see code A) give 6, color 6, or yellow, drop chain, raise left hand to

73

hip, spelling again, pick up chain once more and sp
window, shift weight.

·This last example is given without trying to abbre
ate and is necessarily much longer than could be accor
plished by abbreviations.   We will now give an examp
of code used in abbreviating and which one can follow
improve on to suit themselves.

ABBREVIATIONS.

Class A, animals.	Class B, birds.	Class D, designs.
A, antelope.	C, chicken.	A, anchor.
B, bear.	D, ducks.	C, cross.
C, cat.	E, eagle.	H, heart.
D, dog.	G, goose.	M, maltese cross.
E, elephant.	O, ostrich, etc.	S, star.

G, Geometrical.	H, Houses.	I, Insects.
A, angle.	C, church.	A, ant.
C, cylinder.	M, mill.	B, butterfly.
D, diamond.	T, tower.	F, fly.
E, ellipse.	S, street.	S, spider.
O, oblong.		
S, square, etc.		

M, Man.	F, Fruit Pictures.	L, Landscape.
A, angel.	A, apple.	B, boat.
B, beard, face.	B, banana,	M, mountain.
C, child.	C, cherries, etc.	T, tree.

F, face, etc.   L, lake.

M, Marine View.   If you get a suggestion whispered,
                       say an elephant for example, you face
S, ship.   medium and give C, A, E—C for
L, lighthouse.   class, A for animal, E for elephant,
R, rocks.   etc.
B, little boat, etc.

Test No. 2, drawing of compound pictures—Make a
separate list of abbreviations for the various articles
forming the picture.

After collecting the various suggestions, turn toward
medium and give her in 4, 5 or 6 letters and outline.
The first letter showing whether it shall be a landscape,
marine view, or fruit picture. For example, L. M. L.
H. R., meaning landscape with mountains, lake house
and road. This can be transmitted in about 5 seconds,
medium picks up crayons and makes a rough outline of
picture in black, then turns and while picking up the
necessary colors of crayons gives the details, for example: 2 T, two trees. 3 B, three boats, and in this manner
proceed until the entire picture is finished.

Card Test—If a plain card, left hand hanging.

If a face card, left hand at hip. 1, clubs, 2, diamonds, 3, hearts, 4, spades. 1, ace, 2, deuce, 3, tray,
4, four, 5, five, 6, six, 7, seven, 8, eight, 9, nine, 0 ten,
hand hanging. 1, Jack, 2, Queen, 3, King, hand at hip.
For example, King of spades: place hand at hip, and
give 3-4, the 4 for spades and the 3 for King. For six
of diamonds, hand hanging, give 2 for diamonds, 6,
for six.

75

Coin test.

1—Gold,	2—Silver,	3—Nickle.
—	—	—
1—$1.00,	1—3 cents,	1—3 cents.
2—$2.50,	2—5 cents,	2—5 cent old st
3—$3.00,	3—10 cents,	3—V, or new st
4—$5.00,	4—20 cents,	———
5—$10.00,	5—25 cents,	4—copper
6—$20.00,	6—50 cents,	—
———	7—$1.00	1—one cent.
	— ——.	2—continental c
		3—2—cent new st

The date is given backwards, and the century if
is omitted, if 17, the 7 only, is given, for example a
cent piece of 1863 is transmitted by 2, 6, 3, 6.
first two shows silver, the six shows 50 cents, the tl
is the last and the six the second last figure of date,
would be drawn by medium, reversed. The perfor
explains this by saying, the medium follows the di
tion of my mind, but appears as though all suggest
are not caught as given, but exactly the reverse, i
picture in a mirror, or a negative in a photograph. '.
bluff enables the performer in all such tests where s]
ing is necessary, to give the signs at one time, for
medium standing behind the glass facing performer
does not have to turn around as would be the cas
drawing on the paper. The coin test paves the wa]
the visiting card test, ask for any visiting card and s
the name backwards to medium, first give her two
ters, when she has drawn the first one, or really the

, one, give one more and in that manner keep one letter ahead all the time.

The watch test is similar to coin test, but it is done on the glass.

1-Gold hunting case. 2-Silver hunting case. 3-nickle hunting case. 4-Gold open face. 5-Silver open face. 6-Nickle open face. Left hand at hip if stem winder. Left hand hanging if key winder. Example— Gold open face watch with extra dial for seconds and stem winder, time 4.48. Signs, left hand at hip, stem winder. 4-Gold open face, shaking chain, little dial, 3-4-6, making 4 signs in all. This drawn in reverse on glass which from front will show 12 minutes of 5, gold.

The figures may be omitted in drawing, to save time.

Bank note test: This will hardly need description.

1-equals $1.00,. 2-$2.00, 3-$5.00, 4-$10.00, 5-$20.00, 6-$50.00, 7-$100.00, 8-$200.00, 9-$500.00, 10-$1000.00.

You spell and give the numbers backwards, just the same as in visiting card test, giving the value first.

The whispered word test—This test is executed just like the visiting card test, spell backwards, one letter at a time and written on glass.

Other tests will readily suggest themselves and in fact they are without limit.

The tests should be so arranged that each varies from the one preceeding it. Don't introduce a visiting card and a whispered word test in succession. They are too near alike.

A file of soldiers march out from a line, one on ea side of stage. The one in command takes each gun se arately and hands same to performer who looks throu barrel, then hands same back, until all six guns ha been inspected. Then performer steps to one side stage. The commander now calls for cartridges, ea man takes a cartridge from his cartridge-bag, co mander collects them on a plate, where the soldiers d posit same. They are now handed by the comman to the audience for inspection, and are marked by an ence for identification. Commander collects cartrid on plate goes to stage and hands each soldier a bul The soldiers hold up the bullets till the last moment audience can see them. Commander now orders the out on foot board, about forty feet from performer. Co mander gives orders to aim and fire, which they do ar performer catches the bullets.

Explanation—The Springfield Rifles are "O. K." Th cartridges are fixed, that is, the bullets are only fit into shell tight enough not to come out easily, so as l allow inspection, (people do not generally try to pull the bullet.) Each militia man gets one of these bulle which when order for bullets is given are handed to co mander, he allows them to be inspected, marked, etc then collects same on a plate. As he returns to stage goes as far back as possible, while doing so he chang the cartridges, substitutes cartridges that have wax ti formed like a bullet, coated with plumbago. The so diers hold up these bullets. Audience cannot distir guish but that the bullets are "O. K." These are load into rifles, the effect when fired is same as a blank shot. When commander returns with plate on which bullets have been collected, he leaves the real bullets, which are quickly extracted from the shell and handed to performer, who apparently catches them when fired at him.

45   Head of Ibykus, or Talking Skull.

While your assistant shows the head around to the audience holding it on a platter or server, you put two chairs back to back, a short distance from each other. At one side of stage is a small table on which lies your wand and over the wand lies a strong black thread, both ends of which lead off to your assistant behind the scenes or in the next room. Near this table stands a sheet of glass, which has been ground smooth on both sides. You fetch this, let it be examined, and as you return to stage, place it upright in your left hand, and let it lean against the left shoulder, with your right. hand pick up wand thread with it, lay the hand on the upper narrow side of the glass plate, hold it out in front of you flat, i. e. level, and assistant lets thread loose enough and holds both ends wide apart, so that the middle lies around the right narrow side. As soon as this is done, place glass on the chair backs, pressing it down on the four corners where it strikes the chair sides, on top of which it rests and on each one of same is previously put a little wax so glass rests securely. Now assistant has the thread under control, it goes from his right hand over and across the glass, around the narrow side and

79

back to his left hand, and he can pull it back and for
without its sticking. You now take head, place it
glass behind the thread and take the upper thread, whi
assistant lets loose a little and loop it once around
pin in lower jaw. Now if assistant holds left thre
securely and pulls on the right, the head nods, and if
pulls first one and then the other to and fro, he
moves back and forth on glass. First meaning "Ye
second "no." Now you can put a globe over it to sh
there is no connection, but see that a foot is on
globe or a slit in it, that is towards front, so thread c
move easier. Now of course head answers question
and tells chosen cards, and always looks or turns sid
ways whenever you face audience, but when you face
it faces you or straight ahead as though nothing h
occurred. This always awakens laughter, and final
you catch the head at it, and ask why he is always loo
ing to one side, if his bride is there? And he answe
with a yes. And so on, tells age of person, how man
years before a young lady will marry, if she will
blessed with children, etc., etc., and to last question
keeps on nodding (knocking or rapping) till y
command it to stop, and immediately goes at it aga
Now ask one or two gentlemen to come up and lift t
glass globe and examine all. Before gentlemen g
there, ask the head if he knows them, no. Ask if the
can come up and examine him, yes; and as the
approach, assistant lets upper thread loose, and pul
the lower slowly and quietly, and loop works off the pi
and then pull in quickly so gentlemen can examine.
head is to answer by moving jaw, etc., take out the pi

80

from upper right back of lower jaw, and then jaw moves on pulling the thread.

If head is to smoke, place it on table top, in which are two ferules fitting into holes in bottom of head, from the lower ends of these lead out two rubber tubes, back to assistant. Place a cigarette in left opening between teeth, hold match to it, assistant draws and blows smoke through the other tube, if smoke is not strong enough, assistant has another cigar to smoke, and head quietly smokes the cigarette while you prepare for another trick.

---

46   The Mango Tree.

The rod of the table which may be a glass topped one, contains a piston, to which are fastened or rather hinged, ribs of an umbrella, the whole contrivance lying folded up in the hollow leg of the table. When the string of piston is pulled, the latter raises above surface of table and the hinged arms spread out by their own weight.

The piston rod has branches or arms which are made to resemble branches of a pink plant or rosebush by attaching to them feather leaves and flowers. (Pinks folding smaller than roses are preferable.) The flower flower pot used is a double one consisting of a heavy outside bottomless shell, the inside pot proper being made of tin and filled with sand. After being examined the inside pot is got rid of, leaving only outside pot which is placed on table. In due time the piston raises and under cover of the handkerchief laid over

the pot, the tree expands and visibly grows, till at
it has attained its proper height. It is then shown
the flowers which are detachable, are appare
snipped off and thrown over into a basket, which is
changed for a similar basket of natural flowers, wh
are then distributed to audience.

47　　　　　Queen of Knives.

Have a large block of wood about one foot in di
eter, fasten into the floor or ground, it is about 3
high and round.　Have a knife about two feet long,
inches wide and 1½ inches thick.　(It is made like
corn cutter) with a handle.　This is driven into
wood, the sharp edge, and with a sledge hammer d
it down further.　Have an iron bust (corset) or ap
ratus like the old "Suspension," but it works in
back of lady.　Lady keeps her legs crossed when she
placed on the knife.　The notch must fit "snug" o
the edge of knife.　She wears a fancy "Mother H
bard" dress, with a 4-inch lace collar to hide the
notch.　When lady walks the iron is between her l
It is made long so she can rest when laying on it.

48.　　　　　The Appearing Lady.

On the stage is a platform which is raised above
floor by four legs about 6 inches high.　On this p
form are four uprights, one at each corner, this form

a frame on which to hang the curtains. . Back of this
there is a screen made of red calico. The performer
goes behind the platform and pushes a stick through to
show that there is no mirror, etc., underneath it. The
performer and assistant now prepare to put a curtain
around the frame work. Performer and assistant each
takes hold of the curtain and pull against each other
to show that there is nothing concealed in it. This is
done in front of the platform and conceals a small mirror being dropped under the platform by an assistant
below the stage. It is dropped at an angle to reflect
the bottom of the platform which is covered with the
same kind of cloth as the background. Performer and
assistant take the curtain and place it on the frame
work and form a cabinet. Performer standing in front
holds the curtain with one hand and counts 1-2-3, curtain opens and there stands a lady dressed in white.
She comes through a trap in stage and platform, the
small mirror preventing her from being seen while
ascending. Or have only trap in stage and let her come
in the cabinet through a slit in the back.

---

49.   The Escape From Sing Sing.

For the illusion you have two cages, each 7 feet
high and 4 feet wide and 4 feet deep. Each cage rests
on 4 legs which elevate them eight inches above the
stage floor. The sides and the door have dark red curtains and the back has a curtain of the same color as
the stage is draped with; usually a dark grey to repre-

sent a cell. The sides, front and back of the c
also have wooden rods running up and down. T
are blackened so as to look like iron, they are a
half an inch thick and are set in the framework of
cage about 4 inches apart. Three or four of these
are loose at the back and can be moved so the pris
can come through. Each cage has a small shelf at
back for the assistant to stand on. To work
illusion you require two men dressed alike as priso
and one dressed as a policeman or guard. When
stage curtains go up the cages are standing well
on the stage. Cage number 1 has all curtains up
the performer walks behind this when entertain
Number 2 has back curtain down and as it is of
same color as the stage background, the audience do
see it nor the guard who stands on the shelf behind
Now prisoner number 1 rattles chains in the wings
comes running on stage. Performer stops him at p
of revolver and puts him in cage number 2, and cl
the door and pulls down the curtains. Soon a voice
heard calling, ''let me out,'' performer opens the d
the prisoner has gone and there stands the guard.
this moment the prisoner comes running in thro
audience to stage. Performer and guard seize him
put him in cage number 1, and close doors and d
blinds of both cages. Fire pistol. Open cage door
blinds of both cages and behold the prisoner is seen
cage number 2. You see that when performer p
prisoner in cage number 2, he removes the back b
lets down the curtain and changes place with the poli
man, who raises curtain, puts back bars and then c

to be let out. The other prisoner then rushes in through the audience. Now when they put him in cage number 1, he gets behind the curtain and the prisoner in cage number 2 comes into cage and leaves the back curtain up.

———————

A wire is run across the stage. On it are hung two screens about 7 or 8 feet apart, and about 18 inches above the stage. Screens are plain wooden frames covered with paper or cloth. Behind each screen is placed a stool, the screen hanging about two inches below the top of the latter. The performer gets on a stool behind one screen, and extends his hands to show that he is really there. Then he draws his hands back, and in one instant, he is transferred invisibly behind the other screen. Here he shows both of his hands, and travels in an instant behind the first screen, and then he steps out before the audience.

Explanation:—The frames are covered with paper or cloth, and are hung by two hooks, screen 1 is unprepared. Screen 2 is prepared as follows: It has two stuffed gloves behind it and a cord holding the dummy hands behind the screen, the cord leads behind the stage to your assistant. Performer gets on stool behind screen, extends his arms and shows his hands. Performer now draws in his hands behind the screen, and the assistant slacks on cord and the stuffed hands behind screen 2 drop out of their own weight, and represent the performer's hands. These false hands have white gloves on

85

same as the performer, who has now apparently trav
eled behind screen 2. Now assistant pulls string. Th
causes the dummy hands to fold behind screen 2 an
performer extends his hands from behind screen 1, an
then he steps out before audience.

---

51   **Noah's Ark.**

On stage is seen four uprights, upon which rests a
elegant casket, in appearance of an antique boat; i
the front side of it are two windows. Performer remov
the cover and lets down all four sides to the stage, t
show that nothing is concealed in it; the sides a
closed up again and cover put on. A large funnel i
now placed in a hole in top of cover and the perform
proceeds to fill the casket with water, bringing on pai
of water to do so. After water is poured in perform
opens the windows and takes out a large number of dove
rabbits, ducks, cats and all kinds of articles, etc., the
removing cover, white clouds ascend and a lady is see
rising out of the casket, dressed to represent the rai
bow. This is a first-class sensation, and a sure hit
No mirrors, black curtains or reflections used.

Secret—The front and back and both ends let dow
to show empty. There is a small shelf on back of boa
where girl is. You let front down first, then ends an
back. Front and ends keep audience from seeing gir
on back when it is down. Put back up first then end
and front. Then pour in water and put on the boxes
As soon as front is up girl opens back and connects

rubber hose to end of funnel which is placed in hole on top, the other end she places in hole on top of one of the legs, (all four of the legs are hollow and will hold a large pail of water,) after each pail of water she places rubber tube in different leg until four pails of water have been poured into top of boat. As soon as done girl takes animals out of one of the compartments and places same in box nearest that end and then she takes some out of the other end and then back to first end, and so on until all the things have been produced. Then in due time she pushes up the lid of boat and makes her appearance on top of boat. Lady should be dressed in a very handsome costume.

While performer takes stuff out of one of the boxes girl is loading other box, these boxes form the ends of ark.

----

52   The Oriental Barrel Mystery.

On stage is seen standing a platform about twelve inches high. Performer going behind platform pushes a sword through underneath it in order to show that audience can see beneath it. He then shows an ordinary newspaper and places this upon the platform. He then brings forward a common ash barrel and puts this on top of the paper and platform. He then introduces the young lady with whom he is going to perform the illusion. He gives her a pistol and places her in the barrel, and tells her to crouch down so that he can put the cover on. Performer then asks lady to hold out the

revolver and one of her hands from beneath the cover &
audience can see that she is there all the time. The
barrel is held together with two hoops, one at the top
and one at the bottom, and by a piece of string tied
around the centre. Performer commences to remove
the hoops, the bottom one first and then the top one.
The barrel is now held together by the string only. Lady
is instructed to shoot when he says three. Performer
counts 1-2-3 and at the word "three" pistol is heard, the
barrel falls apart, the lady is gone; audience look up in
the gallery and see lady standing there.

Secret—When performer introduces lady all eyes are
naturally turned upon her and audience fail to see that
a curtain is lowered between the two front legs, by an assistant beneath the stage. There should be a screen of
the same color behind the platform. The barrel platform and stage each have a trap in them so the lady
can go down. The newspaper is also prepared by being
mounted on stiff cardboard and this also has a trap cut
in it. When the performer tells the lady to crouch down
she goes through the trap, beneath the stage and hur-
ries up into the gallery or other place of appearance.
The assistant immediately pushes up, by the aid of a rod
a pistol and dummy hand. The hand is made of a
stuffed glove which is the same color as the one the lady
wears. The performer takes his time in removing the
hoops of the barrel in order to allow the lady opportunity
to reach her place, when he starts to count 1-2-3, the assistant underneath the stage takes in the pistol and
dummy hand and closes the traps. At three the lady
in gallery shoots the pistol. At the same instant the

88

performer cuts the string and the barrel falls apart. The construction of this illusion is as follows: The bottom of the trap is a solid wooden rim with a star trap in the centre, each stave is fastened to this rim with a hinge which helps to hold the staves together when the string holds them without the hoops, but which will allow them to fall outwards when the string is cut. The lady should wear an Eastern costume.

---

53 · The Artist's Dream.

This wonderful and charming illusion is meeting with great success in England. A large frame with a curtain in front rests on a three step platform on stage. Artist pushes aside the curtain, removes canvas with picture of lady on it from frame, turns canvas and frame around to show that no one is concealed anywhere about the frame and canvas. The canvas is then replaced in the frame, curtain drawn in front of frame and the artist seats himself on a chair, apparently goes to sleep and dreams that the picture came to life. While in pretended dream curtain opens and a living lady steps from the frame, artist awakens and sees her: they exchange a few words, then she goes back into frame; artist says, has my model come to life or have I dreamed it. He goes to the frame opens the curtain and there finds only his painted canvas; the lady having vanished.

The canvas with the painting on it is on a separate

frame or stretcher which is very heavy, the top piece of this frame is hollow and contains a roller on which the canvas rolls up the same as the curtain in the watch frame. On the back of the stretcher on each side is a handle, these handles are apparently placed there for the artist to lift the frame in and out by. But they serve another purpose which will be stated below. At the top corners of the stretcher are fastened two wires which lead up to the flies, over a pulley and then down behind the screens to the assistant, when the wires are slack the stretcher may be turned around just the same as if they were not there. The large frame is on rollers and may be turned around to show that there is nothing concealed in or behind it. After showing frame and back and front of canvas artist sets the canvas back into the frame. When the canvas stands on the floor in position to replace, the lady comes up through trap door behind the canvas which conceals the movement, she takes one of the handles referred to above in each hand and places her feet on the lower part of the stretcher which projects enough for her to get a passable footing. The artist now raises the canvas back into the frame. The wires attached to the stretcher are pulled by your assistant, this makes the lifting of the stretcher with the lady on it easy enough. Now all the lady has to do is to unfasten the canvas and let it roll up into the stretcher, she now steps out on the stage from under the curtain. After she goes back she lowers the canvas and hooks it. The artist then pushes aside the curtain and finds only the painted canvas.

In the centre of the stage or on a platform is seen a half lady resting on a wooden horse with 4 legs. The stage or platform must be 4 feet high. The trestle is 3 feet high and $3\frac{1}{2}$ feet long. On the top of the centre of the trestle make a bust like that used in "Swinging half lady" and have it ironed on the trestle and finely finished. Black cloth is tacked to the back of the two rear legs. The walls at the back are draped with the same kind of goods. Have a framework in front and partly over lady, on which you hang curtains. When you open the curtains audience sees the half lady resting on the trestle. The lady is behind the trestle resting on her knees, and leaning against the bust, which should be dressed in some light color. No lights are needed to shine inside as the front curtain hides everything. Have it very dark at back of front curtain and the trestle fastened to the floor.

.

55 Edgar Poe's Raven in the Garland of Thebes.

A fine raven sits in a beautiful garland of roses, suspended in midair by two ribbons, bird talks, sings, whistles and tells fortunes with startling effect. Raven is a fine stuffed bird surmounted by a garland of flowers which is suspended by attaching the silk ribbons to garland at sides opposite the bird's mouth. These ribbons are double and contain a rubber tube, the ends of which are concealed among the flowers. Assistant behind sings, speaks and whistles into a metalic chamber connected with one of the tubes, the sound passing out in a direct line with bird's mouth, apparently coming from it.

* * *

56   Samuel's Cartomantic Floral Charm.

A pack of cards transformed to a profusion of flowers. Secret—A hollow metal fake pack is loaded with spring flowers, (roses) having a loop at end, hanging out, and through which performer passes his thumb, and produces flowers, vanishing pack up sleeve by the usual clip.

* * *

57   Samuel's Mystic Percolator.

A glass percolator (two gallon size) is used for this experiment. Percolator is shown to company perfectly empty, covered with a shallow silver cover, and given to a lady or gentleman to hold upright. A large silk handkerchief is thrown over it to exclude the light. Performer now empties a cornucopia of paper roses, which were a few moments before mysteriously produced from cone, right into tube of his blunderbuss, (large size tube) and shoots flowers into the percolator, where they are found as soon as the handkerchief is removed from it. Flowers are concealed inside silver lid of percolator (on principle of coin cork) so that pressing a small projecting pin on top of cover when throwing handkerchief over it, the trap door bottom gives way and the spring flowers fall out, a spiral spring closing door again.

---

58   Samuel's Wonder Kraut.

A cabbage is transformed to an Aquarium containing live fish. A small aquarium having mouth closed by rubber cap, same as fish-bowl trick, is inserted inside an artificial cabbage, made of cloth, or cloth and rubber, nicely painted to resemble the genuine article. Colored silk handkerchief is thrown over cabbage and both covers removed at the same time.

---

59   Samuel's Magic Squeezers.

Performer, during the performance of some trick, requires a glass of wine, taking a deck of cards in hand he squeezes them tightly several times until a whole glass of wine is extracted from them.

Secret—There is a faked deck, picked up with four or five cards in front to spread out to prove genuineness. Remove pellet of wax or wooden plug from air hole and wine runs out of small hole in bottom of fake. The fake pack is made of tin, having nicely painted edges and real cards glued on front and back. Fill fake with a small fine-tubed syringe. A very effective trick used in conjunction with flying glass of water or wine.

Two tassels hang in any appropriate place on the stage, apparently for mere drapery effect. They are made to resemble the ordinary heavy, every-day tassel, used to tie up heavy curtains, etc., the body of tassel is hollow spun metal of sufficient capacity to contain a full glass of wine. Air hole in top of fake. ‑Plug in bottom drawn out of fake by performer pulling smartly on thread which hangs below tassel, at a very short distance thread is not visible.

An extraordinary improvement can be made by having a rubber tube covered to represent cord, connected with one of these tassels by an opening made in the top of the hollow receptacle. Rubber tube fitting over a hollow metal connection.

---

61 **Samuel's Bloodstone Wonder.**

A large white stone is inspected. Performer remarks that the old adage declares that you cannot get blood out of a stone, but this is now made possible by the charmed bloodstone. Here he taps the stone several times with the hollow metal wand, at third blow wand and stone are lowered over a tray on table and blood pours from the stone into a glass tumbler on tray, blood comes from wand, blood is then vanished by vanishing glass of water, etc. Stone is wrapped in paper and the package exchanged on servante for one containing a loaf of bread of same size, this is placed on run down. Performer fires wand at package, opens it and states that Satan has commanded the stone to change to bread. This bread can contain previously borrowed arricles, or cards to be produced from it.

---

62 Samuel's Handkerchief Tassel.

Tassel is made similar to wine tassel, except a slight alteration in base, this one being perfectly open. When performer desires a large and beautiful silk handkerchief, he simply puts his finger through a loop at end of a silk thread hanging a few inches below the fringe of tassel and while calling attention to something in the air, he makes a downward sweep of the right hand instantly disclosing the handkerchief, flag, glove, etc., silk ribbons or anything else capable of being hidden beneath its mystic recess.   ·

---

63 Samuel's Golden Flash of Light.

A ladies' handkerchief is borrowed, ring for flash handkerchief of same size. Handkerchief is ignited and disappears instantly in a flash leaving in sight nothing but a heap of gold coins in performer's hand. Purchase from Western News Co. a Columbus souvenir pile of gold coins sold for paper weights, attach a cat gut or wire loop to it and suspend it on back of left hand, under cover of flash handkerchief, swing it into palm, when you place handkerchief there to vanish.